LLEWELLYN'S

Little Book of

EMPATHY

Katie Cannon Photography

Cyndi Dale is an internationally renowned author, speaker, healer, and business consultant. She is president of Life Systems Services, through which she has conducted over 65,000 client sessions and presented training classes throughout Europe, Asia, and the Americas. Visit her online at CyndiDale.com.

LLEWELLYN'S
Little Book of

EMPATHY

CYNDI DALE

LLEWELLYN PUBLICATIONS
WOODBURY, MINNESOTA

FIRST EDITION
First Printing, 2019

Book design by Rebecca Zins
Cover cartouche by Freepik
Cover design by Lisa Novak and Shira Atakpu

Llewellyn Publications is a registered trademark of Llewellyn Worldwide Ltd.

Library of Congress Cataloging-in-Publication Data
Names: Dale, Cyndi, author.
Title: Llewellyn's little book of empathy / Cyndi Dale.
Description: FIRST EDITION. | Woodbury : Llewellyn Worldwide, Ltd., 2019. |
   Series: Llewellyn's little books ; #10 | Includes bibliographical
   references.
Identifiers: LCCN 2019018224 | ISBN 9780738760896 (alk. paper)
Subjects: LCSH: Empathy. | Social psychology.
Classification: LCC BF575.E55 D35 2019 | DDC 152.4/1—dc23 LC record
   available at https://lccn.loc.gov/2019018224

Llewellyn Worldwide Ltd. does not participate in, endorse, or have any authority or responsibility concerning private business transactions between our authors and the public.

All mail addressed to the author is forwarded, but the publisher cannot, unless specifically instructed by the author, give out an address or phone number.

Any internet references contained in this work are current at publication time, but the publisher cannot guarantee that a specific location will continue to be maintained. Please refer to the publisher's website for links to authors' websites and other sources.

NOTE: The information in this book is not meant to diagnose, treat, prescribe, or substitute consultation with a licensed healthcare professional.

Llewellyn Publications
A Division of Llewellyn Worldwide Ltd.
2143 Wooddale Drive
Woodbury, MN 55125-2989
www.llewellyn.com

Printed in China

Disclaimer

⧂

The information in this book is not intended to be used to diagnose or treat any medical, emotional, or behavioral conditions. To address social, emotional, mental, medical, behavioral, or therapeutic issues, please consult a licensed professional, such as a therapist, psychiatrist, or physician.

The author and publisher are not responsible for any conditions that require a licensed professional, and we encourage you to consult a professional if you have any questions about the use or efficacy of the techniques or insights in this book. References in this book are given for informational purposes alone and do not constitute an endorsement.

All case studies and descriptions of persons have been changed or altered so as to be unrecognizable. Any likeness to actual persons, living or dead, is strictly coincidental.

Contents

൭

Exercises

Tips

INTRODUCTION

Are you a little frightened?" asked the gray-haired woman seated next to me on the plane.

I looked over, startled. How had she known?

I hate turbulence. After one bump, my hands clench and my stomach knots. I didn't think I'd let on, however, at least not obviously. Rather, I'd pretended to read.

"Don't worry, dear," she said, patting my hand and ignoring my astonishment. "We grandmother types are always on call."

My seat mate had delivered a dose of empathy, the ability to sense what is occurring in those outside of ourselves. Specifically, she'd dispensed emotional empathy, one of the four types of empathy you'll learn about in this book. The other three styles are physical, mental, and spiritual.

In a nutshell, these four capabilities can be defined in the following ways:

PHYSICAL EMPATHY: The ability to sense what is occurring in another's body, including relating to illnesses, aches and pains, and all other types of unpleasant and pleasant sensations.

EMOTIONAL EMPATHY: The capacity to feel others' feelings as though they are our own.

MENTAL EMPATHY: An aptitude for cluing into another's thoughts and perceptions, as well as plugging into the universal mind, a gigantic mesh of knowledge.

SPIRITUAL EMPATHY: The talent for relating to beings in the spiritual realms, including the deceased, entities, angels, and even the Spirit— a higher power by whatever name works for you—as well as the spiritual essence within all living beings.

As you'll find out, any number of living beings are hard-wired for these four empathic capabilities. Groupings include humans and other primates, but also natural beings as far flung as rodents to trees. And we can even empathize with invisible beings! For what reasons is our empathic capacity so available?

Amongst humans, empathy is most well known for establishing social order and relational connectivity, enabling the exchange of love, care, and ideas. But empathy does so much more.

Because of empathy, we can sense what others are internally thinking and respond accordingly. Because of empathy, members of a group, from familial to athletic, can individually thrive. Because of empathy, a mother can respond to her child's unspoken needs, and a friend (and her chocolate chip cookies) can make everything all better. Because of empathy, we can sense what is occurring in the spiritual realms and benefit from our otherworldly connections. Empathy assures us that we aren't alone. Everyone gains when we unite through love.

Empathy isn't always so lovely, however.

Some individuals aren't able to fully activate or employ their empathic circuitry. The "underempathic" are often quietly and sadly left outside the circle of love.

Others twist their empathic skills to get what they want from others. Then there are those on the other side of the coin: the victims of deceit, the individuals whose empathic aptitudes can be manipulated. Too often, they end up indulging others' needs and ignoring their own.

There is one more empathic challenge. I call it "over-empathy." It's the one that has caused me the most difficulties. When I was a child, I was so completely attuned to others' physical conditions, emotional entanglements, and hidden beliefs that I was a wreck. I couldn't tell if I was catching the flu or overidentifying with an ill sister. I didn't know if a bout of sadness reflected my personal feelings or belonged to my mother. I flailed around in confusion if I sensed that a teacher was lying or that a relative was prejudiced. Why did no one else seem to notice? And worse, I was afflicted with an even more unusual empathic conundrum: I was overly conscious of the unseen universe. To me, shadowy entities, angels, and the deceased were as animate as the living. Sorting the supernatural from the natural was an exhausting process. It can be as harmful and isolating to be too "tuned in" as it is to be overly "tuned out."

How can we avoid our under- or overempathic tendencies and also refrain from being manipulative or manipulated? In this book, you'll learn all the concepts and techniques needed to prevent empathic downsides and assure its upsides, the latter including the following:

- increased ability to set and achieve financial and lifestyle goals
- improved bodily and emotional health
- boosted creativity and passion for life
- ease in separating others' feelings from your own
- augmented ability to give and receive compassion
- stronger and more loving relationships
- bolstered self-esteem and self-confidence
- an acute ability to problem-solve
- intensified capacity for perceiving and making the best choices
- a level-headed approach to dealing with toxic people and their beliefs
- enhanced connections to spiritual guides
- heightening of powers needed to reject negative people and spirits

The ideas and tools taught in this book can lead to the just-touted results because they drill empathy down to its foundation. If you want to excel at a skill—and empathy, though innate, is also a proficiency—you have to understand how it works. For all the social and classical science research, which I'll touch on in this book, empathy is essentially an energetic process. To be good at empathy, you must understand and gain a facility with energy.

Energy is information that moves, and absolutely everything is composed of it, including objects, bodies, thoughts, feelings, and spirits. There are two types of energy, however: physical and subtle. This distinction is crucial to comprehending empathy.

Physically, empathy is managed through hard-wired neurons and a complex interaction of biochemicals. Our psychological profile, which is mainly body-based, enables us to send, receive, and interpret empathically delivered information. Subtle information, on the other hand, which is also called psychic, spiritual, mystical, and intuitive data, composes the bulk of the information we emanate and take in empathically. In other words, empathy produces concrete results but mainly occurs through the exchange of unseen information. Our vulnerability to being too empathic, underempathic, involved in manipulation, or just plain confused empathically occurs if we're unaware of what is happening in the subtle realms.

Comprehending this point will leap you ahead in your use of empathy. Being able to sort the data you want to pay attention to versus that which is useless or even harmful will deter any tendencies toward empathic problems. It will also enable you to enhance your present-day empathic traits and activate untapped empathic styles. All this is possible because of one of the major teachings presented in this book: the need for empathic boundaries.

Empathic boundaries are sheaths or rings of invisible energies composed of your own subtle energy. These boundaries determine the input and output of empathic data. As a baseline, you must have empathic boundaries. They provide you the safety needed to accelerate empathically and the softness required to relate to others. Hence, you will find that a lot of the exercises and tips provided in this book enable these boundaries and also show you how to react if they are compromised.

As a note, I teach two of the techniques featured in this book, which are Spirit-to-Spirit and Healing Streams of Grace, in many of my other books. If you're already aware of these processes, you'll love learning how to directly apply them to your empathic gifts. If these processes are new to you, I believe you'll come to depend on them as much as I do in all empathic endeavors. In fact, not only do I use these two favored techniques in my personal and professional life, but I also employ the other practices taught in this book. They've made a monumental difference in my life.

I can now go shopping and keep track of my agenda, no longer swayed by the lists in my fellow shoppers' minds. I can sit at the doctor's office, concentrate on my own aches and pains, and not be awash with others' bodily complaints. I can relate to another's emotional reality without losing track of my own and notice the presence of a spirit and decide if I want to connect or not. In other words, I can be empathic and still be *me*.

Professionally, I've learned to empathize with clients while simultaneously accessing insights and information. In fact, as an intuitive counselor and energy healer, I've accomplished these goals with over 65,000 clients. I can sense and often alleviate areas of physical and emotional discomfort without becoming exhausted by the end of the day. I can tune into a client's hidden thoughts without being washed away in a cascade of mentality and accurately assess the nature of the spiritual beings that a client is associating with. I can also help a client release harmful spiritual forces so they can better bond with beneficial ones.

If you'd like to do the same empathically, but in your own way, the following is a layout of the chapters that will enable you to constructively employ your empathic gifts:

CHAPTER ONE: **Laying the Groundwork.** Here we'll cover the basics for healthy empathic engagement. You'll learn about the many assets of empathy, how empathy operates energetically, how empathy can work for and against you, and about the need for empathic boundaries. I'll also reveal the many different types of beings you can associate with empathically and fully describe the four main types of empathy.

CHAPTER TWO: **Filling Your Toolkit.** The five different tools featured in this chapter will be applied in the following chapters. They will aid you in activating and using your empathic abilities and also in establishing appropriate empathic boundaries.

CHAPTER THREE: **Physical Empathy.** Physical empaths are so physically porous that they can often absorb or take on others' bodily sensations and symptoms, even to the point of smelling, tasting, or touching what others are experiencing, as well as feeling others' physical pain. Conversely, if too shut down, a physical empath might close off opportunities for physical bonding and the reaping of material abundance. This chapter will more fully describe the physical empathy gift, as well as research about it, and show you how to safely relate to others' bodily concerns.

CHAPTER FOUR: **Emotional Empathy.** The innate drive for emotional connectivity enables bonding, relating, and compassion, but can also lead to codependency and other challenges. The tips and techniques in this chapter will help you more fully embrace the world of emotion while resisting "emotional contagion," an overinvolvement with others' feelings, or, conversely, the self-protective stance of shutting down to others' emotions.

CHAPTER FIVE: **Mental Empathy.** Also called cognitive or intuitive empathy, mental empathy allows us to gain perspectives that are meaningful to ourselves and others. At best, this ability aids us in becoming wise and learned and enabling the same in others. At worst, we can become overrun with our own or others' fantasies and judgments or be unable to relate to another's point-of-view. In this chapter you'll learn how to appropriately enhance this special ability while remaining independent and nonjudgmental.

CHAPTER SIX: **Spiritual Empathy.** Through spiritual empathy we relate to the essence in both living and supernatural beings. Examples of the latter include the deceased, spiritual guides, angels, negative entities, and any name you use for the Spirit (such as God, the Universe, the Holy Spirit, the Goddess, Allah, and the like). In this chapter you'll learn how to assess the nature and motivations of worldly and otherworldly beings, free yourself from negative forces, and use your empathy to embrace a soulful life.

CHAPTER SEVEN: **Healing and Manifesting.** Shhh—not many people know that empathy can be employed for healing and manifesting. Well, now that the secret is out, you'll love learning how to apply empathy toward these vital ends. Various exercises will aid you in helping others (and your-self) clear roadblocks from the past, evaluate current life situations, and manifest desires. Each exercise will blend all four empathic gifts so you can practice using them simultaneously.

In the end, I believe that this book can become your roadmap to the penultimate goal of empathy, which is to give and receive love.

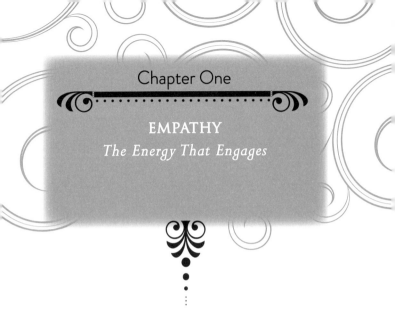

Chapter One

EMPATHY
The Energy That Engages

Empathy is key to engaging with others in healthy, vibrant ways. It allows connection, bonding, and compassion. It promotes increased creativity, new perceptions, and spiritual support. In short, it is the energy that makes the world go around, while keying us into what's happening in the world.

In this chapter you'll learn all the basics required to ease your way into the most exciting relationship adventure possible: the development of your empathic gifts. In order to lay the groundwork, I'll start with more fully defining empathy while exploring its four major types, which are physical, emotional, mental, and spiritual. I'll outline the various benefits afforded the empathic expert and the reasons that we benefit from consciously developing our empathic abilities. In short, when our empathic faculties are distorted, there are lots of downsides, hence the need for training as well as empathic boundaries.

Everything empathic is easier to perform upon understanding how empathy really works. The short answer is "energetically." Empathy involves the exchange of energy between two or more beings. After exploring this topic, I'll further delineate between two types of energy, which are physical and subtle, and showcase the different ways our physical and subtle systems enable empathy. Add to this a laundry list of the various beings you can empathize with, and voilà, you'll be ready to fully activate your empathic powers.

The Power of Empathy

When I think about the powers afforded us through empathy, I'm reminded of William Blake, one of the most famous English poets. Most likely you've read the first few lines of his well-known poem "The Tyger":

Tyger, Tyger, burning bright,
In the forests of the night;
What immortal hand or eye,
Could frame thy fearful symmetry?

The poet continues to wonder how the same creator that formed the tiger could have also made the lamb. How can these two opposing beings coexist? Furthermore, how can our own tiger and lamb natures coexist?

Our tiger self is wild, feral, passionate, and totally self-oriented. Our lamb self is kind, gentle, caring, and ready to assist others without concern for the self. Empathy blends both aspects of ourselves while encouraging the same in others. At least, that's what happens when we perform empathically in a healthy way.

Our tiger self is dedicated to personal survival. While empathy involves relating to others, the smart empath never, ever endangers their own physical, psychological, or spiritual well-being. The challenges of empathy, described in the introduction as overempathy, underempathy, and manipulative tendencies, are averted if we remain aware of our personal needs, even while offering concern for others.

Our lamb self relaxes our boundaries so we can attune to others. When we resonate with another's physical, emotional, mental, or spiritual reality, we can "walk in their shoes." We can accommodate their innermost sensitivities and lift them into a good space.

The fully empowered empath is both a tiger and a lamb, devoted simultaneously to personal security and another's welfare. This balance requires both conceptual and practical education, and, above all, an open heart. It enables us to be the way we are created to be: a tiger and a lamb, caring for self and other.

As you'll learn in this chapter, the "other" might be another person. Then again, an empathic subject might be an animal, natural being, or supernatural entity, such as the deceased or an angel; it might even be an aspect of yourself! But before we meet our possible empathy partners, it's imperative to better understand the four basic empathy styles, which I'll describe with examples:

- You are sitting across from a friend at a coffee shop and your knee starts throbbing. You wonder if you banged it that morning. Then your friend says, "My knee is so painful that my doctor is suggesting a knee replacement." All along, you were physically empathizing with your friend's pain.

- Your mom is frowning but you can't help but feel like she's hiding something that makes her happy. Later you find out that your sister is pregnant and your mom wasn't letting on until your sister could tell you. Your emotional empathy was right on.

- Your co-worker says that he likes his job, but your gut insists the opposite. You weren't at all surprised when he quit the company to return to school. In the future, you vow to put more faith in your mental empathy.

- You feel creepy around your brother. There is something shadowy surrounding him. Finally, he says he thinks he's affected by a dark spirit. Your spiritual empathy was on point.

Respectively, each of these four examples provides a picture of physical, emotional, mental, and spiritual empathy, which I more completely distinguish in the following ways:

PHYSICAL EMPATHY: Sensing in our body what is happening in another's body. When our body operates as an empathic medium, we might feel another's sickness, pain, healing state, or any other physical condition, including a positive healing sensation, as if it's our own. For instance, when sitting in a movie theater, you might actually think you're being kissed or shot when the same befalls a character.

EMOTIONAL EMPATHY: The awareness of another's feelings in your own system. When your emotions are stirred by another's emotions, you'll feel their anger, fear, disgust, sadness, or joy. You might also simultaneously sense your own feelings. Imagine that you were promoted but a fellow employee, a friend, wasn't. You can be happy for yourself and still also be sad for your friend.

MENTAL EMPATHY: The ability to understand another's thoughts, beliefs, and perceptions, and also pull information from the universal mind. Quite typically, this data is relayed as a gut sense. Let's say that you easily sense when another person has a surprise for you or someone else. Blurting aloud your awareness is a certain way to ruin that event, whether it's a birthday celebration or good news. Your ability to sense what's on another's mind is a sign of mental empathy. So is the power to tap into the universal mind, a sort of "computer in the sky." You know you're on target when a light bulb goes off and you simply know the answer to a problem.

SPIRITUAL EMPATHY: The facility for associating with the spirit or essence of a living or other-worldly being. Through spiritual empathy you might attune to a person's inner essence and subsequently become conscious of their true talents, value system, or spiritual needs. You might also affiliate with a ghost, demon, angel, or the Spirit itself. As well, you might relay a message to someone from an invisible being. For instance, I once sensed that a client's deceased brother was telling her she'd survive a hard divorce. She knew it was him because the message included a vision of a man singing and cooking; he did both professionally when alive.

Some spiritual empaths can also get rid of negative entities or beings. I have a friend who can sense dark presences around her clients; she feels them as hovering figures that turn her stomach. She then uses divine energy to free people from them. Her clients almost always report an improvement in their lives.

Are you excited about the broad range of empathic abilities? Their benefits are even vaster than my short snapshots reveal.

Why Empathy?
Let's Count the Reasons

Empathy formulates the bonds that support individuals within a social compact, but the gains of empathy don't stop there. Empathy produces dozens of extraordinary outcomes for the empathizer, the subject of the empathizer, or both. In short, empathy does the following:

- *Makes us feel good.* Relating to another person (or being) lights up the pleasure centers of the brain, filling the empathizer with joy molecules and good will (Center for Building a Culture of Empathy, n.d.; Light and Coan 2009).

- *Enables conflict resolution.* When we resonate with what others are saying, feeling, or thinking, as well as with their essential selves, we build bridges instead of walls. In response, the person being empathized with gains clarity about their beliefs and possibly might be better able to relate to our own.

- *Provides perspective.* We become broader minded when we work on understanding why someone believes or acts the way that they do.

- *Encourages expression of values.* Most religious and spiritual persuasions uphold virtues such as compassion and altruism. While empathy allows us to assess whether another's values are aligned with their behavior, it also issues an invitation to look in the mirror. Are *we* living conscientiously?

- *Inspires receptivity.* While empathy involves giving to someone else, it also encourages us to receive another's empathic concern when it's needed.

- *Enables better relationships.* Relationships blossom and grow when both parties are aware of what each other is experiencing.

- *Improves health (under the right conditions).* The subject of empathy can experience decreased stress, including the release of emotional strain, also making for easier problem-solving. The same can occur if we're the empathizer, except when we overidentify with the stricken. In this case, our stress levels leap off the charts (Ratner 2017).

- *Brightens an emotional state.* Studies show that people who improve their empathic skills enjoy a more positive attitude toward life and undergo fewer negative emotions and emotional strain (Panayotova 2017).

- *Leads to better health outcomes.* Research has shown that patients treated with compassion and empathy respond better to medications and other treatments; as well, empathic practitioners make fewer mistakes and are themselves happier and healthier than non-empathic practitioners (Stone 2016).

- *Fosters creative expression.* When others support our unique gifts, relating to our passions with excitement, we are more apt to share ourselves with the world and reap the resulting rewards. When we support another's special qualities, we're encouraged to fire up our own innovative goals.

How can we not look forward to delivering or garnering these and the many other results of empathy?

Key to providing empathy is having already undergone what another is going through. In fact, research underlies this point (Bergland 2013). This means that it's far easier to relate to someone if we've experienced a similar joy or challenge. It's harder to empathize if another's situation differs from our own, but it's still possible.

I should know. I'm a mother of boys.

I differ from my sons in more ways than I can count. Obviously, I'm female. But both sons are extremely athletic, and I'm one of the least sporty persons I know. Oh, I walk my dogs and lift a few weights, but especially in comparison with my youngest son, who is a college-level baseball pitcher, I'm a sludge. The last time I threw a weighted baseball, the type used for pitching practice, it rose a few feet and smashed my foot. I limped for days. One of my dogs scooped up the ball and carried it away, seemingly rolling his eyes at my lack of ball savvy.

Nonetheless, because I'm physically empathic, I always know when my baseball-playing son has pulled a muscle, sometimes even before he's aware of the injury. Half the time I've already made an appointment with the appropriate body worker before he brings up the pain. I'm also fully attuned with his emotional reactions to a game well (or not-so-well) pitched. Hence, I'm ready with the right post-game comments. And, above all, I'm tuned in to his ultimate goal, which is to follow his passion to the nth degree. Because of empathy, I can play faith-holder, ball girl, financier, and cheerleader.

Empathic Pitfalls and Pit Stops
Distortions to Avoid

As with all aptitudes, empathy is rife with snares and obstacles. There are three basic empathic dangers that might occur if your empathic abilities become distorted. Falling prey to any of them can stop you from reaping the empathic benefits described in the last section.

Succinctly, the three categorical distortions are being overempathic, underempathic, and either manipulative or manipulated. See if you can relate to any of these conditions as I explain them. In chapters 3 through 6 we'll more thoroughly examine the dark sides of all four styles, as well as the reasons that they might happen.

Overempathy

Overempaths are easily overwhelmed by others' physical, emotional, or mental realities, or by their awareness of the unseen world. Respectively, symptoms include becoming flooded by another's bodily concerns, illnesses, and desires; pleasant or unpleasant emotions; or perceptions, judgments, opinions, and knowledge. You can also be overtaken by the concerns, values, and consciousness of another's core self, which I call their spirit or essence, as well as the invisible spirits involved in an empathic process. These additional spirits are usually spiritual guides, but they also can be the spirits related to individuals—alive or dead—who participated in an event. For instance, if you are checking in on a friend who is sad, you might get a sense of their spiritual guides as well as the spirit of a person who caused them grief.

Social scientists often apply the term "contagion" to describe the hyper-empathic condition in which one person's state of body, mind, or soul catches fire in another.

In fact, a single person's turmoil can infect an entire group. This is what happens when a single frightened person in a crowd creates a mass panic.

The overidentification with another's situation is often a result of "empathic absorption." We'll use this term frequently in this book. Basically, absorption occurs when we soak up and hold onto so much of another's empathic data that we lose track of our own bodily needs, feelings, knowledge, or value system. Caregiver personalities are especially susceptible to this mistake, which can lead to caregiver burnout and its many afflictions, such as exhaustion, illness, depression, inflammation, and a lack of interest in life.

Sometimes a person so overempathizes that they become rather unlikable. That's right! We can become so concerned for another that we walk right over their boundaries in order to "help them." For example, I have a client who constantly complains about her lack of friends. When I probed for the reason, she said, "They just don't know what's good for them. I keep telling them, but they don't listen." No one likes being smothered or bossed around, and it's not good for us to be codependent, or to do for others what they need to do for themselves. And when overrelating to others' issues, we don't have to deal with our own.

Another overempathizing trait is called projection. When projecting, someone puts their issues and ideas on another. We project in minor ways all the time, such as when we stub our toe on a dresser and then yell at the dresser. It's actually our own fault we walked into it! Overempaths usually over-own others' projections. For instance, because they take on issues that aren't their own, they can end up acting out another's ignored feelings, aches and pains, and even discriminatory attitudes. I once worked with a client who was always upset. Her boyfriend had absolutely no feelings about anything. I told her to only feel her feelings, not her boyfriend's, and showed her a few of the techniques in this book, namely those in chapter 4. She immediately stopped overexpressing, and within a few days her boyfriend began complaining about feeling emotional.

Actually, I believe that overempathy is a common and very understated problem underlying many of the afflictions attributed to physical or psychological conditions. I once worked with a twenty-five-year-old client afflicted with rheumatoid arthritis and an insatiable sex drive that he said didn't feel like his. On the positive side, he displayed an uncanny ability to predict the rise and fall of stocks. He simply sensed how others would react to changing economic conditions and bought and sold stocks based on these intuitive perceptions. Though young, he was well on his way to becoming wealthy.

It was obvious to me that my client was a physical empath, exhibiting the positive and negative qualities related to physical empathy. As we'll further explore in chapter 3, the signs of being a physical empath center on relating to the world physically, factors that include the body and also the obtaining of material needs. This made me wonder if my client was acting out other peoples' issues.

"My mom does have arthritis," he admitted. "And I think that my dad had affairs when I was young."

I explained that physical empaths can absorb and reflect energies from others in order to assist and heal them or ease tensions in a family. Using the techniques presented in both chapters 2 and 3, I helped my client release his mother and father's energies, sending them to the Spirit to be dealt with in a loving way. However, I encouraged him to retain his financial acumen. His investment intuition qualified as a healthy use of empathic skills. Within a few short months, my client's arthritis had disappeared. He was dating a lovely person and was continuing to make good money at stocks.

Underempathy

Underempaths are partially or fully blocked in at least one type of empathy. An underphysical empath can't relate to another's physical concerns. For instance, even if they are aware of another's physical injury, they might not understand why the wounded person can't run fast or keep up with their lives. Emotionally, the underphysical empath often exhibits a low affect, which means that they struggle to convey their emotions or relate to another's feelings. This can lead to being seen as cold or uncaring.

Empaths who score low on the mental or cognitive scale are often unable to relate to another's perceptions, thoughts, or beliefs. This can therefore come off as overly naïve, "out of it," or only concerned about their own beliefs and opinions. And individuals who are underspiritual often have no idea why someone's religion, spiritual expression, or value system is important to them. They might also be so unaware of their own inner sense of the Spirit that they mock those who believe in a higher power.

Low empathy is sometimes caused by a genetic predisposition. For instance, individuals on the autism spectrum carry DNA traits that make them empathically challenged. Because of this, they inherently labor to figure out what others feel or need.

Some underempaths can show feelings and appear empathic but are faking it. Quite simply, they mimic others without relating to them. While the cause might be genetic, it can also be the lack of role modeling or a psychological issue, namely psychopathy.

Psychopathy is a personality disorder characterized by a lack of empathy or remorse. Most typically, psychopaths are responsive to their own pain but not to another's pain. In fact, during a study, when highly psychopathic people imagined that they were in pain, their brains lit up in the same fashion as occurs when someone is empathizing with another person. These areas in the brain did not activate in the psychopath, however, when someone else was in pain. In other words, psychopaths can empathize with themselves but not others (Bergland 2013).

Being underempathic isn't a life sentence, nor should it be considered a social disease. As I'll discuss throughout this book, there are steps for stirring a sleeping empathy, although therapeutic coaching might also be needed to address any deep-seated challenges.

Emotional Manipulation

The term "empathic manipulation" applies to those who misuse their empathic sensitivities to get what they want from others, as well as the individuals who are easily steered by empathic schemers. Either activity points to misunderstandings about love. Manipulators don't comprehend the benefits of loving another person, and the manipulated aren't clear about the importance of self-love.

Empathic manipulators often fit the character descriptions of the "dark triad," people characterized as narcissists, Machiavellians, or sociopaths. I'll examine each category in terms of their empathic skills or lack thereof, but first I want to qualify my comments.

At one point or another, we're all guilty of manipulation. I remember knowing exactly what to say to my father when I was a child to get him to give me more chocolate-covered cherries than he would my sisters. They were his favorite treat. If I said they were also my favorite, he would sneak me extras. Both my sons would say they were too tired to clean their room; I know I did the same myself.

It's natural for children to test boundaries. As adults, we sometimes use manipulation without knowing it when coping with difficult situations. In fact, sometimes it's just plain smart to do so. I have a client who reports to a perfectionistic boss. My client knows that if she makes her business reports look a certain way, with the "right" layouts and fonts, her boss will pass them through, often without reading them. Otherwise, the reports will be stuck untended for days and my client will fall behind in her work. The simple use of manipulation once in a while doesn't make us members of the dark triad. Rather, those afflicted with empathic manipulation are continual manipulators caught in a pattern that causes them great relationship challenges, if they are unaware of them.

Narcissists are self-focused individuals whose inflated views of themselves leave no room to care about others' desires and feelings. Quite simply, other people are fodder for their own needs.

Typically, narcissists are considered underempaths. Since they care only about themselves, they see no reason to relate to another's physical needs, feelings, thoughts, or spiritual well-being. In my own experience, however, I've met many narcissists who are actually quite empathic. The issue is that they misuse the perceptions they pick up from others, playing to another's empathically conveyed needs in order to get what they want.

Machiavellian personalities are individuals who have no problem breaking rules in order to prosper. Typically, it is thought that Machiavellian personalities bypass empathy and are consequently incapable of connecting with others. However, research shows that Machiavellians are actually mentally empathic but not emotionally empathic. Thus, they use their intuitive and observational faculties to figure out what to say and do, but they lack the capacity to care how others feel about their often rude and cruel actions (Taylor, n.d.).

Sociopaths are rule breakers. They are easily agitated, prone to outbursts, and don't feel guilty about their violent deeds. Since they are unable to form attachments, we would expect that they would be underempathic, but the truth is that they are often highly empathic. For instance, they can sense what they are putting another person through, but they don't know how to adjust their behavior accordingly.

Sociopaths are "made" by negative life experiences, in contrast to psychopaths, who seem to spring out of the womb ready to charm their way through life. Thus does science usually argue that genetics create a psychopath and the environment forms a sociopath (Bonn 2014).

What about the other side of manipulation?

Unfortunately, it's quite commonplace for the lambs of the world, especially in contrast to the dark triad tigers, to be misused by manipulative empaths. For instance, I worked with a client married to a narcissist who was recovering from hip surgery. She waited on him hand and foot, but at some point the doctor insisted that her husband start taking care of himself. "The exercise is good for him," stated the physician.

My client's husband was still in a little bit of pain, but boy, did he overplay it. His wife, however, who couldn't stand to let him feel bad, continued to serve him—until she had a nervous breakdown. Basically, the husband used his wife's physical empathy to avoid getting back on his feet.

Sometimes the easily manipulated empath isn't aware of their tendencies and simply requires education. Other times they have bought the line that to be a good person requires obliging everyone else and ignoring the self. And some manipulated empaths lack self-love. Usually, this issue arises because childhood safety depended on taking care of others' needs, to the detriment of the self. These can be hard issues to untangle. While you'll learn exercises to help clear the reasons for these types of propensities in chapters 3 through 6, I'd encourage you to work with a licensed professional if a problem is deep or persists.

As an aside, it's also true that manipulative people can sometimes be unaware of their tendencies and patterns. A narcissist might be copying dad's behavior; a sociopath might lack the interpersonal skills necessary to act in less violent ways. It's important to remember that education and instruction can be a vital tool for nearly anyone on both sides of the manipulation coin.

My own point of view is that empathy is available to everyone, but there are many reasons for its blockage or overresponsiveness. These include childhood wounding and abuse, unrecognized autism spectrum conditions, lack of empathic modeling and training, and being rewarded for being manipulative or manipulated. As well, some individuals with attention deficit disorder (ADD) can appear nonempathic simply because they struggle to focus. In actuality, the opposite is really true. I find that most ADD individuals are very sensitive.

As I'll explain, empathy is even more an energetic process than a social one.

It's All About Energy

Succinctly, empathy is the engagement and exchange of energy between two or more beings.

Energy is information that vibrates, and it composes absolutely everything. There are two major types of energy, however. Physical energy is measurable and concrete. It is regulated by classical science, which suggests that if you set a fork on a table, it will stay there until actively moved. Subtle energy, on the other hand, is immeasurable. Also called psychic, spiritual, mystical, intuitive, and quantum energy, subtle energy obeys an entirely different set of rules, or lack thereof.

Subtle energies are governed by the laws of quantum mechanics, which are quite unlike their classical counterparts. Take that dinner fork. Whereas the physical energies will remain in place unless disturbed, the fork's subtle energies are constantly flickering in and out of existence. Not only that, but they can be directed by conscious will. This means that if you really focus, theoretically you can make the fork disappear and turn it into a spoon. After all, as Albert Einstein insisted decades ago, energy doesn't disappear; it merely transforms. Alter subtle energies and the physical appearance of them can change.

One of the reasons that subtle energies are so malleable is that they are really tiny. Called quanta, these are the most minute bits of data in the universe. Quanta are so small—and fast—that while traveling, they can actually be in two places at the same time, and, in fact, in any one of the scientifically known and unknown dimensions simultaneously. In addition, once two quanta—or objects, people, or other energies, have once been involved, they will continue to affect each other, even when separated by time and space.

What do all these subtle rules and regulations mean for you as an empath? As you'll discover in our next two sections, empathy is a very physical endeavor. It employs the physical body and is highly predictable. If you've sensed others' fear before, you will again. If a friend constantly picks up on your aches and pains, the same will happen next time you're injured. As predictable as subtle energies are in this way, they are also highly creative.

Out of the blue, you might be hit by an emotion and have no idea who it belongs to. You could be suddenly felled by the flu and wonder if it's your own or if it belongs to someone unknown. You might sense an invisible presence and either be helped or harmed by it, or predict a friend's cancer and send them for testing just in time to save their life. In other words, because of the subtle energetics involved in empathy, you can reap gains that go far beyond those available only through the physical mechanisms of empathy.

The Physical Dynamics of Empathy

Scientists have known for years that the mechanics of empathy are hard-wired in the physical body. Simplistically, there are three basic ways that we connect to others from a biological point of view. The most well known is through mirror neurons.

Mirror neurons are a specialized type of brain cells that help us mirror another's state of mind and emotions. If another person is in physical agony, our pain receptors turn on; same with fear, joy, and other feelings. In fact, these nerves exist in all primates, not only in people. Through our mirror neurons, we can also watch another's gestures, postures, and facial expressions and figure out what is happening inside of them. We know how important mirror neurons are in relation to empathy because people with empathic challenges, such as sociopaths and psychopaths, are deficient in mirror neurons, and the consequences on those around them can be painful and hurtful. As well, individuals on the autism spectrum, as well as persons with social, motor, and language problems, also lack mirror neurons, but their effects on others aren't "inhumane." They are simply people whose brains are different and require specific types of assistance and training to cope with the challenges of everyday life (Lehrer 2008).

A second and very important explanation of the empathic exchange of physical energy is the existence of electromagnetic fields (EMF). It's been well-established that we are composed of oscillating fields of EMF, or light. Our DNA vibrates with tiny biophotons or mini units of light, as do all our cells. In addition, every cell, organ, organ system, and the body overall generates fields of light, as does the earth, sun, animals, plants, and just about everything else. Plain and simple, much of our empathic sharing occurs through the exchange of data via EMF fields.

One particular research organization, the HeartMath Institute, has actually proven that people, and even people and animals, exchange empathic information through our EMF fields every time our heart beats. HeartMath is also showing that people can transfer data to and from plants. In fact, when we pick up on what is happening with a tree, we become more positive feeling (HeartMath

Institute 2016, 2019). The fact that EMF fields overlap and interconnect is an obvious way to explain the sharing of empathic data.

A third and recently emerging field of empathy study centers on synesthesia, which occurs when two or more senses are neurologically partnered in the brain. For instance, someone with synesthesia might feel a specific emotion when perceiving a color or hear a tone when touched in a specific way. A specific type of this activity, called "mirror-touch synesthesia," will be discussed in chapter 3, as it shows why some people can sense what another person is physically feeling (Gregoire 2017). Overall, people with synesthesia are typically more empathic than those without it. Over time, we might discover that the brains in overempaths are simply able to call up two or more types of empathy or sensory responses at the same time.

The Subtle Dynamics of Energy

While empathic exchanges almost always use our bodies, the majority of empathic exchanges involve subtle energy exchanges. Because they are regulated by the rather off-beat rules of quantum mechanics, it's hard to figure out what these subtle energies are doing, as well as where they come from and what we're supposed to do about them. Yet it is vital to be able to accomplish these goals, which is why we need to comprehend the mechanics of subtle energies.

In a nutshell, the process occurring in subtle energy exchanges is similar to that involving physically empathic data. Both happen through an anatomical system. The main difference between the physical and subtle systems is of visibility.

As you know, the physical anatomy is made of organs, channels, and fields, but so is the subtle anatomy. The main subtle organs are the chakras. The subtle channels are called "nadis" in the Hindu esoteric system and "meridians" in Asian healing traditions. And the most well-known subtle fields are called the auric fields; each is an extension of a specific chakra.

Chakras outshine and outperform the physical organs in regard to empathy because they can process both physical and subtle energies. In fact, they are able to convert physical energy to subtle energy and vice versa. This means that they have their "hands" on every bit of data that an empathizer picks up.

The job responsibilities of the chakras are also heftier than those of their physical kin. While physical organs regulate only physical concerns, each chakra also manages a unique set of physical as well as psychological and spiritual concerns.

I work with a twelve-chakra system. Seven are located inside the body and five outside of the body. In addition to their basic activities, every chakra also processes a unique spectrum of subtle frequencies. These frequencies can be organized as empathic messages. In other words, each chakra is a master organ and officiates a certain type of empathic information. In fact, a number of different chakras band together to regulate the physical, emotional, mental, and spiritual empathic styles.

The subtle channels running through the body also play a role in empathy. Basically, the subtle channels move empathic information from one chakra and related bodily site to another. In the meantime, the auric fields, independently and collectively, act like a filter system. Based on the programming in a chakra, the related auric field will decide what empathic data can enter the system, how it will be interpreted, and what empathic messages will be shared with the world.

The auric fields are incredibly important empathically. Just think about it: if you believe you should feel everyone's feelings, the related field will absorb everyone's emotions. If you think it's smarter to deflect everyone's emotions, you can work on the oft-unconscious programs that have turned you into a sponge and begin establishing better energetic boundaries.

This portraiture is a fundamental explanation for why we're all different when it comes to our empathic sensitivities. Basically, our programming—composed of ideas formed in childhood, other lifetimes, and taken in from our family and culture—is stored in the chakras, which, in turn, "tell" our auric fields what empathic data to let in or disseminate. These chakra-based beliefs also inform our physical energy or EMF fields, which are also involved in empathic exchanges, although they aren't the only source of our physical programs. In general, our empathic programs might be working for us. Then again, they might not be. The conclusion is that if we want our empathic gifts to operate at an optimum level, and decrease our vulnerability to the empathic downsides, we have to maintain healthy empathic fields.

The Need for Empathic Boundaries

Empathic boundaries are the filters that decide what empathic information we will let in or disseminate. These sieves are composed of our EMF and auric fields, among others, and so they can be considered both physical and subtle in nature. The controlling programs are also physical and subtle, consisting of the ideas stored in our neurological system, including the brain, and our subtle system, specifically the chakras.

We'll look at the specific types of programs affecting the four different types of empathy in chapters 3 through 6. In each of those chapters, I'll also show you how to cleanse and transform the related empathic boundaries. At this point, however, I mainly want to emphasize the importance of these boundaries, which enable you to accomplish the following:

- ***Register, not absorb, another's empathic data.*** We've already discussed what can happen when we absorb or take in and hold onto another's empathic information. It's far more effective to simply register information, which involves simply sensing a message before releasing it once it's understood. Registering rather than absorbing assures us that we'll never confuse what is our own rather than another's concern. It's much safer to simply sense that another person is in pain rather than allow that pain to take up residence in our own body. It's much better to allow the sensations to disappear as soon as we're done analyzing them. (We'll more fully discuss the issue of registering versus absorbing in chapter 2.)

- *Separate our personal issues and sensations from those belonging to others.* It's vital to differentiate between our physical issues, feelings, knowledge, and consciousness and the same in others. When we don't, we can too easily become empathically overwhelmed, able to be manipulated, or codependent.

- *Reject unhealthy empathic information.* Just because we can empathize with what is occurring in others doesn't mean it's good for us to do so. For instance, I don't allow my empathic fields to take in energies from sadists or psychopaths. You'll learn how to arrive at your personal rules of operation throughout this book.

- *Release energies that are not your own.* Empathic boundaries don't only prevent problems, they also help us release them. Many of us learned to inadvertently take in others' energies and keep them inside. Many of the exercises in this book will help you pinpoint, get rid of, and shake out these energies.

- *Establish a time table.* Do you really want to know what a friend, relative, or worse, a stranger is going through in the middle of the night? It's okay to have an open-and-shut-door policy. Various exercises in this book will show you how to establish your rules.

- *Emanate securely.* We have a right to our privacy. There are times when I don't want anyone else knowing what is occurring in my body, mind, or soul. My boundaries can create a sacred space so I'm not exposed to manipulation. Ways to do this will be shown throughout chapters 2 through 6.

Beings Everywhere

Any of the four empathic styles can connect us to a plethora of various beings, which can dwell across all time and space. In order to help you negotiate these beings during the following chapters, consider the following short list:

Living People

You can potentially connect to any person in this world, whether or not you know them. Of course, it's far easier to be empathic with someone we know, or if we are physically empathic, to people who are near us. It's also simpler to understand another's feelings, knowledge, or spiritual linkages if we have experienced a situation similar to the one they are going through.

As well, we can also interconnect with an aspect of a living person (or any being, for that matter), such as an inner child or part of the soul. For that matter, we can connect with a part of ourselves, such as a self who was emotionally wounded during childhood or became injured during a past life. You'll be shown how to relate to yourself empathically at several points in this book.

Living Natural Beings

Depending on your personality, you can potentially sense the empathic realities of any living natural being. This can include animals, reptiles, fish, and the like; plants, trees, and other such organisms; and even rocks and stars.

I've had clients who have reported the distress of a tree being cut down in their yard or of a rock being shorn in half on a mountain. In Peru, where I've often studied with shamans, I can touch a plant or flower and accurately perceive its medicinal qualities.

The Deceased

Ghosts are souls that linger in the earthly realm after death. Constituting this grouping are people who have passed but also the deceased souls of animals, foliage, and the like.

Many people connect with people who have died. My own father recently visited me, although he died nearly thirty years ago. I was driving to a baseball game in Arizona and I suddenly felt his presence in the passenger seat. Although I couldn't see him, I sensed his presence through my physical empathy. My emotional empathy then kicked in, and we both cried because we'd missed each other.

Many people report visits from their deceased pets, and yes, even trees and plants. One of my clients can feel the presence of an oak tree she used to climb as a child whenever she was scared. Another tunes into "Mama Cow," a family cow that he'd spent a lot of time with as a child. He'd always felt that she was more a mother than his human mother.

Otherworldly Beings

There are unlimited numbers of otherworldly beings that we can link with. This list is especially important to consider if you are spiritually empathic. I share it so you know you aren't "crazy" if you are inclined toward these connections:

OTHER-DIMENSIONAL AND PLANETARY BEINGS:
There are constellations in multiple dimensions that host beings who can communicate with us. Many of my clients experience this grouping. Recently, a young male client of mine reported sensing the presence of an alien girl sitting near him at the movies. After attuning to her, he could psychically see her. She was blue in color and wanted to tell him that she would help him achieve his life purpose.

MASTERS, AVATARS, AND ASCENDED MASTERS:
This category includes beings from earthly and otherworldly realms who are more advanced than most humans and are tasked to assist and help us. For instance, I have a client who communicates with a being he calls "Master Light." This master fills him with awareness of higher knowledge. My client has written down these mentally provided empathic messages and published them.

ANGELS: There are many types of angels standing ready to assist us. At one time or another, almost everyone I've ever worked with has suspected they were attended by an angel. Angels report directly to the Spirit and can communicate with us through every form of empathy.

DARK ENTITIES: There are souls that seek to prey upon the living, including people, animals, and other types of natural beings. I call them dark entities, dark forces, or interference. In order to remain associated with the earth, they use manipulation to steal energy from the living. Mainly, they seek to steal their victim's life energy, which is the power that keeps all living beings alive. They also scheme to obtain light energy, which composes the spiritual vitality that bonds us with the Spirit. I believe that these types of beings often affiliate with people in the dark triad, which were discussed earlier in this chapter, to coax them into serving their will. They can then steal the energy from the victims of the dark triad and use it for themselves. You'll learn how to recognize these beings and release yourself from them in chapter 6.

If you want to get a sense of how you empathically recognize information, see tip 1 on the following pages.

And now it's time to gather the tools needed to further delve into the four types of empathy.

TIP 1

ତ୬ଚ

Which Empathic Style?

What's the easiest way to distinguish between the four types of empathy, which are physical, emotional, mental, and spiritual? Assess a bodily awareness next time you're feeling empathic and ask yourself which of the following statements best applies:

1. I'm aware of a pleasant or unpleasant physical sensation in my body, and it doesn't seem to originate with me.

2. I'm having an emotional reaction, and I have no personal reason to feel these feelings.

3. My perception of a situation is strong, but I have no logical rationale to know what I know.

4. I'm sensing a spiritual presence or spiritual knowledge.

Which number did you select? Your cheat sheet follows:

1. *Physical empathy:* Sensing another's physical condition in your own body.

2. *Emotional empathy:* Feeling another's emotion as if it is your own.

3. *Mental empathy:* Gaining a perception that doesn't come from you.

4. *Spiritual empathy:* Becoming conscious of a spiritual entity or knowledge from outside of the self.

You can test yourself for these types of empathy anytime you desire.

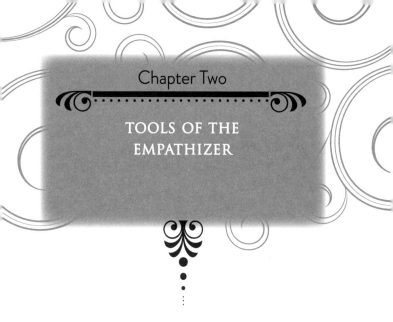

Chapter Two

TOOLS OF THE EMPATHIZER

In chapter 1 we established the need to cultivate our empathy and empathic boundaries. There are specific tools that will enable both activities. Best of all, you can use these techniques on an everyday basis, over and over again.

This chapter features the five tools most vital to empathic endeavors. The two most fundamental exercises, which I recommend using no matter what's occurring empathically, are Spirit-to-Spirit and Healing Streams of Grace. There are three additional exercises that can be used if needed, such as to make sure that you don't hold on to another's energies. These techniques are Registering Empathic Data, Releasing Another's Energy, and the Art of Empathic Mirroring. Not only will I share these techniques, but I'll accompany many of them with supplemental tips. Along the way you'll learn even more about absorbing and registering (two concepts introduced in the last chapter) and the upsides and downsides of mirroring, the act of copying what an empathic subject is displaying.

Spirit-to-Spirit

If there is a one-size-fits-all empathic tool, it's Spirit-to-Spirit. In regards to empathy, I use it to relate to all four types of empathic information, decipher the meaning of incoming data, separate my own perceptions from another's knowledge, decide what I'd like to share with others, and perform just about any empathic communication. If you want, you can even use it to empathize with a part of yourself!

What do I mean by the latter comment? As briefly explored in chapter 1, an aspect of ourselves can get stuck in the past, such as in a childhood issue. You can employ Spirit-to-Spirit to connect with that part of yourself just as easily as you can with other people. You'll apply this knowledge in subsequent chapters in relation to the various forms of empathy.

The most salient question right now is this: How can Spirit-to-Spirit perform so many activities? The answer is that Spirit-to-Spirit allows us to interact with only the highest and best aspects of ourselves and others, and it also invites the Spirit to run an empathic process. To achieve that state, you undertake three steps.

Step One: Affirm Your Personal Spirit

This first step of Spirit-to-Spirit, affirming your individual spirit, activates your own spark of divinity. By putting that essence in charge of an empathic interaction, you guarantee that you'll only operate from love and grace, limiting the possibility that you'll interact from ego or a lower, "wounded" self.

It's easy to perform an affirmation. An affirmation is equivalent to making an inner decree. To formulate an affirmation, you could kinesthetically sense your inner greatness; picture a flame, dove, or another spiritual icon; or simply state your intention silently or aloud.

After affirming your spirit, empathic undertakings will achieve the following:

- be healthy and safe for you and others
- create optimum empathic boundaries for you personally
- invite the same for others, whether or not they consciously understand this
- allow you to follow the Spirit's agenda rather than your own
- enable you to best decipher the gathered empathic information

It seems so simple—and it is! I once worked with a massage therapist whose practice was dependent on her physical empathy, which she used to sense where a client required massage based on the sensations in her own body. The problem was that she was highly overempathic. At the end of the day, she would reverberate with others' aches and pains and was too worn out for a personal life.

The first day she used Spirit-to-Spirit, upon affirming her own Spirit, a warmth surrounded her body. The pleasant heat saturated her skin, and for the remainder of the day, she found herself able to sense her clients' physical symptoms, but they didn't remain in her body. She never again held on to others' physical conditions.

Step Two: Affirm Other Spirits

This step of Spirit-to-Spirit effectively performs two activities. The first involves acknowledging the essence of the person or being to whom you are empathically relating. The second is to verify and sort the presence of any invisible beings that are present. If these beings are negatively predisposed, you'll be able to perceive them so you can deal with them—a process shared through many exercises in this book—or they will be automatically taken away. If they are positive and supportive, they will be enabled to provide appropriate input.

While this step brings out the best in others, it doesn't stifle their lower or more human traits. Rather, it highlights their most honest and light-filled characteristics. Because of this, you'll be apt to pick up only the most truth-filled and accurate empathic messages.

One benefit of this step is that it can protect you from a manipulator's agenda. For example, I once worked with a man who was horribly stressed by his girlfriend. He was very sensitive and kept empathically sensing her inner sadness. Because of that, he never confronted her obviously challenging tendencies, which included using opioids and constantly lying to him. After learning Spirit-to-

Spirit, he was able to sense the rage secreted under her sadness and become aware of her passive aggressiveness. She refused to change, so he quit the relationship, though it was painful for him to do so.

As the story depicts, my client was an emotional empath, but he'd only tuned in to the feelings that his girlfriend consciously or unconsciously wanted him to sense. Step two of Spirit-to-Spirit allowed her spirit to showcase her darker qualities. Now able to gauge her emotional problems, my client became more empathically realistic, understood she was not willing or able to change, and stepped out of his codependent pattern. He also entered therapy to assess the reasons he was emotionally gullible and tracked the issue back to a similar pattern he engaged in with his mother. Eventually, my client entered a relationship with a woman whose emotions matched her words and actions. At this point, his emotional empathy became a gift, as he could use it to relate to a partner who had integrity between her actions and feelings. In turn, she cared about his feelings, which was a fresh experience for him. When he and this partner had challenges, both were willing to alter any unhealthy behaviors, a true sign of relationship health.

Step Three: Affirm the Spirit

The third step of Spirit-to-Spirit is the most important. When acknowledging the Spirit, you surrender yourself and the entirety of an empathic process to the Spirit. In charge of the empathic interaction, the Spirit will show you what you need to know, separate you from energies that aren't healthy to connect with, assist and soothe all parties involved, share the most accurate empathic interpretation, and assure the highest possible outcome to any endeavor.

Will you feel a difference in your empathic relations if you employ this step? When I teach this step to a class, every single person in the audience senses the presence of the Spirit. Some become conscious of a higher power, while others hear words or see visions, but everyone experiences the embrace of a greater goodness.

Now it's time to practice these three steps.

• EXERCISE 1 •

Conducting Spirit-to-Spirit
for an Empathic Interaction

I've designed this exercise so you can implement it while actively interacting emphatically with another person or being. It's also effective if you're reviewing information gathered previously but haven't yet had time to analyze it. For instance, imagine you picked up a message during school or work. You can return to that occurrence and analyze it as if in real time.

While you might know the source of an empathic message, you don't need to. For instance, imagine that you're on a bus and become overcome with an emotion, or you're sleeping and become filled with a sensation unrelated to your dreams. Spirit-to-Spirit will assist you no matter what you know or don't know.

STEP ONE: **Prepare.** Take a few deep breaths and probe into the empathic data. Undergo a quick assessment so you can typecast the empathic message as follows:

- If the information is a part of your body, it qualifies as physical empathy.
- If the data is feeling-based, it is describable as emotional empathy.
- If the message is mental, it is certifiable as mental empathy.
- If you are aware of a higher awareness, truth, or invisible presence, you are using your spiritual empathy.

- If there is a blend of styles or if you are confused, simply acknowledge that this is the case. If you feel overwhelmed by the medley of empathic senses, the next steps will assist you in sorting those out.

STEP TWO: **Affirm Your Own Spirit.** Focus on your heart area and know that you are, and always have been, a divine spark of light. Sense, see, or otherwise acknowledge this truth, and decide that during this undertaking, you'll only operate from this higher self.

STEP THREE: **Affirm Other Spirits.** Focus on your subject. If you don't know the source of the empathic message, your affirmation will embrace that being anyway. Also affirm the otherworldly beings that are present for you as well as those associated with the subject. You are only going to interact with the most divine aspects of everyone and everything involved with the empathic message.

STEP FOUR: **Affirm the Spirit.** Surrender the empathic process to the Spirit. From this point on, the Spirit—which you might picture, sense, feel, or hear from—will manage the rest of the exercise.

STEP FIVE: **Further Analyze the Message.** Focus on the empathic sensation. Review your initial impression of the message. Does it still seem primarily physical, emotional, mental, or spiritual? Is it a mixture of any or all four styles? If composed of a medley of styles, request that the Spirit package them together and then focus you on one style.

Request next that the Spirit cleanse the energies you're receiving and separate your issues from those of the empathic source or any of the attending invisible spirits. Then ask that the Spirit better define the message. Concentrate on the resulting sensations, emotions, or awareness, as well as all related psychic images and verbal insights, until the subject's empathic message is clear. If you are muddled, request that the Spirit make the message obvious at a later date or simply release you from the process and assist the empathic messenger in another way. But if you are clear, ask if you should speak aloud to the subject or otherwise communicate your summarization of what you're empathically concluding. If the subject isn't present, simply ask the Spirit what you are supposed to know or do with the received information.

Ask the Spirit to provide you further inspiration or insights if they are needed.

STEP SIX: **Close.** When finished, ask the Spirit to fill you and all involved parties with the light of goodness. Return to your everyday life when ready.

ॐ

Empathizing in the Moment

Sometimes we only have a moment to respond to someone else's needs, feelings, or knowledge, or to deliver a supportive statement or act of kindness from a spiritual source. How do you pull off Spirit-to-Spirit when under pressure?

After you've received an empathic message, take a deep in-breath. While doing so, affirm your own spirit and all other spirits, seen and unseen. On the next exhalation, surrender the process to the Spirit. Then hold your breath for just a moment and ask that the Spirit decipher the empathic message. Take another in-breath and ask the Spirit to speak through your mouth, thus responding to the empathic information with and for you. Take a few additional breaths and deliberately use the out-breaths to release any undesirable energies, such as the subject's issues or emotions, and thus become purified.

Healing Streams of Grace

Healing Streams of Grace, which I also call "the streams" and the "healing streams," are beams of energy made of grace, which is love in motion, or love that creates more love. Always available, the streams need only be summoned to assist you or anyone and anything else with absolutely any need.

The easiest way to understand these streams is to picture them as beams coming off the sun. The Spirit/ sun creates and nourishes these streams, customizing them for any concern. When called upon, the appropriate streams attach to the needy. There they will remain, transforming when necessary, until the required change is complete.

I constantly employ healing streams during my practice and personal life. To me, they are the most powerful instrument for transformation I've ever worked with.

Typically, I employ Spirit-to-Spirit before I request the Spirit for healing streams. This means that the streams will be directly delivered by the Spirit and that only the Spirit will determine their function. The fact that you aren't involved in targeting and managing the streams for others helps prevent you from becoming codependent or getting overinvolved.

In a nutshell, I recommend that empathic connoisseurs call upon the streams for any of the following reasons:

- ***To assist whomever or whatever you are empathizing with.*** Healing streams can improve their physical health, soothe emotions, adjust perceptions, release a negative spiritual force, or support a spiritual truth.

- ***To separate your issues from another's issues.*** Healing streams distinguish your body sensations, feelings, knowledge, and essence from those of others.

- ***To send a request.*** Maybe *you're* in need of a bit of empathy! Healing streams broadcast your own message to the outside world.

- ***To activate an underempathic ability.*** Perhaps you're blocked in one or more of the empathic areas. The streams can knock down blocks but also erect appropriate filters so you can be reached.

- ***To calm an overempathic capability.*** If you're oversensitive to others' subtle energies, healing streams will forge empathic boundaries by bolstering your EMF and auric fields.

- *To stop manipulation.* The streams can weave strong empathic parameters to keep you from falling prey to manipulators and also prevent you from deceiving others.

If you want an example of how the streams work, imagine you're picking up another's prejudiced thoughts, which is a form of mental empathy. You simply "know" that they don't approve of you because of race, creed, or some other reason. After conducting Spirit-to-Spirit, you might request that the Spirit surround both of you in healing streams, thus establishing energetic parameters. The streams, directed by the Spirit, might now accomplish any number of activities. It might completely block you from the other's nasty attitude. Then again, it might alert you to the deeper reasons why they are so discriminatory. Either way, the Spirit will care for both of you.

The following exercise will help you employ the streams yourself.

• EXERCISE 2 •
Summoning Healing Streams of Grace

Healing streams of grace are available for all circumstances and types of beings. This exercise is designed to be used when you are empathizing. You can also employ it while thinking about an event from the past that you've yet to interpret.

STEP ONE: **Conduct Spirit-to-Spirit.** Always initiate healing streams by performing Spirit-to-Spirit, affirming your personal spirit, others' spirits, and the Spirit, which will manage this process.

STEP TWO: **Assess for Healing Streams.** Review the empathically received information and decide if either you or the empathic subject requires assistance. You will know if healing streams are needed if any of these conditions exist:

- you are overwhelmed with sensations
- you can't get a sense of what the other person is really going through
- you are feeling manipulated or like you want to manipulate

- you or the subject are uncomfortable or in distress
- you sense the subject needs healing
- you're unable to understand the received empathic information
- there is a negative presence or energy impacting you or the subject
- you sense boundaries are being violated
- you're aware of a block in yourself or the subject

STEP THREE: **Request the Healing Streams.** Ask that the Spirit customize healing streams for all concerned. The Spirit will select and fashion these streams and attach them to whomever or whatever requires assistance. The Spirit can also form cocoons of grace around you or anyone or anything else that will serve as protective sheaths. The Spirit will govern these streams in the moment and over time.

STEP FOUR: **Close.** When you feel finished with the healing streams, thank the Spirit for the assistance and ask that it release you from the empathic engagement. The streams will remain operative for you and all concerned for as long as necessary. Return to your world when ready.

Registering, Not Absorbing
When We Take In Too Much

Several times I've discussed how important it is to avoid absorbing and holding on to others' energies. Why do I emphasize this point? Plain and simple, we can't process energies that aren't our own. When stuck in our body, another's subtle energy can create inflammation, physical disorders, warp our feelings, cause a challenging emotional state, distort our thinking, confuse our mind, and connect us to spiritual ideas or entities that are unhealthy for us.

So, what are you to do? As I already shared in chapter 1, the key to clean empathic relations is to register, not absorb, another's energy. What's the difference? I'll give you an example before sharing exercises you can use to accomplish this goal.

Casey the Client
An Example of a Human Sponge

As I've shared in the last chapter, we can attune to all sorts of beings, including animals. Sometimes our pets absorb our energy, and sometimes we take in their energy. My client Casey, a bright little girl, soaked up the issues of her aging pet, Max.

Casey was ten years old and Max was eleven, which meant that she had known Max, a huge Dalmatian, her entire life. Since she was tiny, Casey had ridden on, slept with, and played with Max, her best friend.

About a year before I started working with Casey, Max was diagnosed with cancer. By the time I met Casey, Max was lethargic, tired, and covered with tumors. During that time period, Casey had also become increasingly sad. But she was also stricken with problematic symptoms that made no sense. She was exhausted, and her skin was speckled with strange red bumps. Medical tests revealed absolutely nothing.

When Casey's mom asked me what I thought was occurring on the energetic realm, I suggested that Casey might be a physical empath. I believed that because of her love for Max, Casey might be absorbing and experiencing some of Max's problems. With the mom present, I explained this possibility to Casey, who agreed.

"Yes, I have Max in my body!" she exclaimed.

It made sense. Casey cared about Max. Why wouldn't she unconsciously attempt to carry his illness for him, in an attempt to make it better? I subsequently conducted

Spirit-to-Spirit and asked that streams of grace be sent to Casey and Max so that each could be assisted.

During the session, Casey felt the streams enter her body and relieve her of Max's energy. "It's like he's being lifted out of me," she said.

From that point on, Casey could sense or register what Max was going through, but his problems didn't become her own.

Over the next week, Casey's symptoms faded away. About two months later, Max passed away. Since then, Casey's health has been perfectly normal. Casey has also said that sometimes she feels Max sleeping with her at night, even licking her face.

"He's now my angel," she insists.

Casey had been absorbing Max's illness. Worse, she'd been holding on to it. Because her system couldn't process his energies, they created symptoms in her own body. When she started to register instead of absorb his energies, she could still sense his condition while remaining separate.

As I further explain these concepts, along with mirroring, another important empathic tool, you'll see exactly how important they are, especially toward assisting you in avoiding the pitfalls of empathy.

The Fine Points of Absorbing and Registering

All empathic engagements employ our neurological system, which uses physical energy so we can relate to what others are going through. Even if we're interacting with a part of ourselves, such as an injured inner child, we relate to that aspect of ourselves via our nervous system. But all empathic processes also involve bringing others' subtle energies into our system.

This taking in or absorbing of subtle energies isn't bad. It's sometimes the best way to really "get" another person or being. The healthiness of our empathic endeavors is determined by how much energy we let in, how long we hold on to it, and if we're able to register or "read" the energy instead of keeping it.

In general, the more energy we absorb when empathizing, the more intense our experience and reaction. The better we'll understand another's experience, and the more thoroughly we'll be able to express our empathic comments. I find that the greater another's struggle, the more energy I take in. For instance, when I'm working with clients who were wounded as children, I absorb quite a bit of their trauma. I know that their tiny child self needs to be fully embraced and understood if they are to heal.

Although I might be "one" with another's traumatized self, however, I don't lose myself in the process. I only touch the subject's empathic sensations, holding their energy for a split second. I don't retain it, and because of this, the empathic communiqués slip out of my system as quickly as they slid in. In other words, I register this energy instead of completely absorbing or owning it. Once I've assisted the client, I'm done. I move on to other aspects of a session or my life.

You might suspect that overempaths are more prone to holding on to another's energies than are underempaths; that is not necessarily true. Sometimes a person becomes an underempath because they have taken in so much external energy that they simply shut down. I also believe that some manipulative empaths are stuffed with stored empathic data. As we discussed in the last chapter, sociopaths are made, not born. Imagine what it's like to grow up in complete chaos, perhaps surrounded by physical, emotional, and verbal abuse. One survival instinct is to take in others' disturbed energies and to then discharge them in fits of rage, hence the actions of a sociopath.

Being empathic is complicated. To really use your gifts in an optimum and safe way—and to avoid the pitfalls of holding on to another's energy—you need to know how to absorb, briefly register, and then release the energy. The following exercises will help you gain these skills.

• EXERCISE 3 •

Registering Empathic Data

How do you register instead of absorb and hold on to another's empathic message? These brief steps will give you control over the process and should become your baseline for most empathic undertakings.

To best learn, select a friend to practice this exercise with. Either the subject can be available in person or over the phone; empathy works no matter what. Once you are interrelating with the empathic subject, conduct these steps:

STEP ONE: **Prepare.** Ask the subject to internally reflect upon an event they would like you to understand. The experience might have affected them physically, emotionally, mentally, spiritually, or any combination of the same.

STEP TWO: **Conduct Spirit-to-Spirit.** Before tuning in to the subject, affirm your spirit, the subject's spirit, all helping spirits, and the Spirit.

Give permission for the Spirit to be in charge of this empathizing exchange. You can either state these steps aloud or do so silently. (I recommend the latter, as this is what you'll do most often in everyday life.)

STEP THREE: **Subtly Attune.** Before asking the subject to verbally share their experience, invoke healing streams. These streams will lift the empathic messages from the subject and infuse them into your physical and subtle systems. Review the four major ways of empathic knowing and determine what the other person is going through. Is there a physical, emotional, mental, or spiritual component (or a mixture of the four) to what you are receiving?

Assess your personal reaction to the incoming information. Check to make sure you aren't being under- or overempathic or compelled to manipulate or be manipulated. If any of these events are present, ask the Spirit to wrap you and the subject with healing streams so as to adjust the interaction. The Spirit is in charge and will easily establish the correct empathic boundaries.

STEP FOUR: **Attune Through Sharing.** Ask the subject to speak aloud about the situation for which they are seeking understanding. Ask questions as you feel prompted and also see if you pick up additional physical, emotional, mental, or spiritual messages. Are these empathic sensations stronger or different than those you received during step three?

Then share aloud what you're perceiving. You can use terms like, "I sense you're going through…"; "I feel that you are experiencing…"; "I believe you are thinking…"; "I feel led to share…"; "I relate to…"; and other such phrases.

Also ask the subject for feedback. How accurate was your empathic assessment? Is there anything else they'd like to share? Continue interacting as long as the discussion seems productive.

STEP FIVE: **Release the Subject's Energy.** Ask the Spirit to use the healing streams invoked in step three to cleanse you of the subject's energies. This will help you release all absorbed energies. Congested areas will seem sticky or heavy and will be washed clean. The subject's energies will be

returned to their spirit with love and kindness. If
you need further assistance with this process, use
the next exercise, "Releasing Another's Energy."

STEP SIX: **Close.** Thank the subject for participating
in this exercise. Then you can both return to your
everyday lives.

• EXERCISE 4 •
Releasing Another's Energy

Sometimes we discover that we've been carrying another's energy around for a while. Either that or we find ourselves struggling to disengage a subject's energy during
an empathic experience. During this exercise, you'll
practice letting go of long-stuck energies and your reasons for holding on to them. You can employ the same
process during a live-time empathic event, so remember
the steps.

STEP ONE: **Prepare.** Take a few deep breaths. Think
about a past empathic experience during which
you absorbed and held on to energy that wasn't
your own. Mull over this event for a moment or
two.

STEP TWO: **Conduct Spirit-to-Spirit.** Affirm your spirit, all the spirits that were involved in the empathic exchange, and the Spirit. Return your focus to the empathic event.

STEP THREE: **Review the Empathic Experience.** Ask the Spirit to walk you through the empathic experience and to pinpoint the exact moment you absorbed the empathic information. (If you are walking through these steps in current time, you'll actually be in that experience.) You might sense a physical or subtle area that feels heavy, sticky, agitated, overwhelmed, tingling, or otherwise uncomfortable.

STEP FOUR: **Probe the Decision to Hold On.** Now analyze the reasons why you decided to actually hold on to, instead of release, the empathically received data. Did you believe that you had to? If so, what circumstances created this belief? Is the core perception a survival instinct or an expression of care? Let the Spirit highlight the belief or events that led to your overinvolvement.

STEP FIVE: **Analyze the Effects.** What negative effects have you experienced (or are you experiencing) in response to the stored empathic data? Have you suffered physical issues, such as a recurring pain, illness, numbness, or inflammation? Was your reaction emotional, such as the experiencing of repetitive or bothersome feelings or a seeming inability to sense your own emotions? Are the costs mental? These might be experienced as repetitive thoughts or the inability to let go of a negative perception. Spiritual consequences can include a lack of self-worth, low self-esteem, or the sense that a dark force or entity is plaguing you.

STEP SIX: **Ask for Healing Streams of Grace.** Now that you're cognizant of the energies in storage, it's time to ask the Spirit to take these energies away. Request that the Spirit employ healing streams to release them from you. Remain in this process while you sense, feel, hear, or watch these streams clean out the subtle energies that aren't your own. The scrubbed energies will be returned to the other's spirit, to be reclaimed by them in a safe and gentle way. The Spirit will also replace any empty areas left within you with the appropriate energies.

STEP SEVEN: **Receive the Wisdom.** Now ask the Spirit to show you the wisdom gained through this experience. Ultimately, we cannot do for others what they must do for themselves. The ultimate lesson for you will involve a version of this truth.

STEP EIGHT: **Close.** Thank the Spirit for the assistance and continue with your day.

Mirror, Mirror, On the Wall

Besides understanding the issues related to absorbing, holding, and registering, the empathic expert has to comprehend another important empathic activity, which is called "mirroring." There are two ways to mirror an empathic subject. The first is to let yourself as fully as possible become the subject both neurologically and subtly. The second is to physically duplicate at least some of the subject's behaviors.

We've explored the initial steps of the first method, which is to register another's empathic data. As we've said, you register empathic data by taking it in and briefly sensing it. To mirror neurologically and subtly, you hold on a bit longer and give yourself permission to imagine that you are not only relating to the subject, you *are* the subject. This is a form of mimicking I call "internal mirroring."

The second type of mirroring is physical and involves actively copying the subject's actions. For instance, if the subject is leaning forward when crying, you would lean forward as well, letting them know that you "get their pain." You could even tear up. If the subject itches their ear when they're perturbed, you do the same, informally letting them know that you aren't judging their anger. Be careful, though. You don't want to substitute physical mirroring for full-on empathy. Manipulators often do this, leaving the subjects wondering if they are being understood or played. Only use physical mirroring as an adjunct to a more involved process.

Mirroring is such an important topic that I'll next lead you through an exercise that will enable you to practice both types of mirroring.

• EXERCISE 5 •

The Art of Empathic Mirroring

As explained in this chapter, mirroring another person internally can greatly enhance an empathic subject's experience of being understood—and make sure that we really understand them! We can mirror internally, or through registering and "walking in their shoes," and also via our bodily behaviors.

To ethically and safely perform both maneuvers, which is the goal of this exercise, you must do the following:

Remain conscious of yourself.

- Manage the amount of empathic energies you absorb, which you practiced doing in exercise 3, "Registering Empathic Data."

- Let the Spirit manage the process. This will keep you from overplaying your hand or attempting to rescue the subject.

If you want to practice both forms of mirroring—internal/registering and behavioral—during the same empathic session, line up someone to practice on. I recommend that you interact in person since over the phone you can only physically mimic the subject's voice.

STEP ONE: **Prepare.** Settle into a shared space with the subject. Ask the subject to ruminate internally about an event they would like you to empathically understand.

STEP TWO: **Conduct Spirit-to-Spirit.** Affirm your spirit, the subject's spirit, the presence of all helping spirits, and the Spirit. Give permission for the Spirit to be in charge of the empathizing process.

STEP THREE: **Register Internally.** Ask the subject to communicate about the important situation that they are thinking about and give permission for the Spirit to deliver the related physical, emotional, mental, and spiritual subtle energies directly and safely to your neurological and subtle systems via healing streams. The streams will make sure that you sense and mimic only the energies that are beneficial for you to experience. Now imagine that what you're feeling is actually your reality—that you are going through the experience in the same way as your subject is. When you're ready, state aloud what you are experiencing and ask the subject if they've been feeling the same.

If you feel uncomfortable in any way, request that the Spirit adjust your neurological and subtle systems via the healing streams. If you start to lose yourself, request streams and regain a better sense of yourself. You can also ask the subject what it's like for them to have you relating so deeply with them. Are you on point? Does the intensity leave them assured or nervous?

If the subject relays any discomfort, ask the Spirit to deliver healing streams directly to them or between you, creating more empathic boundaries. If either of you wants to shut down the internal mirroring process, request that streams separate and restore your individual anatomical systems. Otherwise, continue your empathic interactions and conversation and then conduct the following step.

STEP FOUR: **Copy with Your Body.** Ask the subject to continue speaking aloud about the topic. While they share, deliberately mirror a few of their actions. If they lean forward, do the same. If they touch their hair, do so as well. Then point out that you did this and ask the subject how your physical mirroring is affecting them. Do they feel supported or awkward? Does the physical mirroring further enhance the internal mirroring or not? Adjust any physical mirroring until the subject is comfortable with it.

STEP FIVE: **Wind Down.** When finished, close the conversation by leaning backward, thus easing off the physical mirroring. Ever so slowly, ask the Spirit to cleanse the subject's empathic messages from you with healing streams and to send these energies back to the subject's spirit with an infusion of love and light.

STEP SIX: **Close.** Thank the subject for honoring you with their truth, and return to your everyday life when ready.

TIP 3

❧

Internal Mirroring in a Moment

There are times when we sense that someone has an immediate empathic need but we're not in a position to spend time listening to them or talking with them. For example, imagine that you are in a supermarket or sitting on a bus and you sense a person near you is grieving. You can take these steps:

STEP ONE: CONDUCT SPIRIT-TO-SPIRIT.
Before performing any empathic activity, even if you aren't going to speak, always affirm your own spirit, the subject's spirit, all assisting spirits, and the Spirit.

STEP TWO: CREATE A BUBBLE OF GRACE.
Ask the Spirit to use healing streams to form a bubble of grace. The Spirit will place an aspect of the subject in this bubble, which you will sense or psychically perceive in front of you. While the subject is being encapsulated, request that you also be surrounded in healing streams.

STEP THREE: RELATE TO THE SUBJECT.

Request that the Spirit transfer a part of your consciousness into the subject's bubble. This part of you is surrounded in its own cocoon of healing streams so it will be safe while visiting the subject. At this point, this aspect will register or internally mirror the subject's experience or empathic need and send its awareness back to the "greater you," which is operating in the "real" world. If any words need to be shared, the Spirit can speak them through the greater you, even while healing streams continue to pour into the subject. As soon as you've relayed the message, ask that the Spirit reintegrate the part of you that was in the subject's bubble. Healing streams will separate your physical and subtle systems from the same in the subject and then completely restore and boost both of your energetic fields. You'll then be returned to your everyday self.

STEP FOUR: FEEL GRATEFUL.

Be grateful for all the ways you were able to positively affect the subject, and continue with your life journey.

Chapter Three

PHYSICAL EMPATHY
The Body as a Mirror

W e're now going to personalize the empathic process for one particular type of empathy: physical
empathy. Physical empaths can sense what is happening
in another's body as if it's occurring in their own. Case
in point: your friend sits across from you and scratches a
mosquito bite. Pretty soon, you're doing the same, even
though you weren't the one camping last weekend. Or
maybe, when you're on the phone with your dad, your
stomach starts churning. Soon into the conversation, you
discover he has a flu bug.

In this chapter you'll learn all about physical empathy. First, I'll share a few stories that will clue you in to this capability. These examples will reveal the broad array of people, beings, and even objects that are implicated in physical empathy, as well as the many benefits and downsides afforded the physical empath. Then we'll explore the fundamentals of physical empathy. We're always more empowered to properly employ and enjoy a mystical gift if we know how it works—and that it actually does work. And then, after outlining a few key signs of physical empathy, I'll present several techniques and tips enabling the safe and powerful development of your physical empathy.

Without further ado, let's begin.

The Physical Empath
The Body Reveals

We are spirits, but we are experiencing this world through a physical vessel. This means that our "body temple" is just as important as our soul and mind.

More than any other empathic type, the physical empath is aware of the vital role played by the body in the dance of life. You are the person who attunes to the environment, knowing what is happening to everything from animals to plants. You can smell, taste, feel, and be touched by the bodily sensations occurring within other people. And you might even wax and wane with the tides of the moon or hold a talisman and relate to its owner.

Here's a more thorough set of physical empath examples:

- You're wandering in the woods and spy a bird with a broken wing. Your shoulder immediately feels inflamed.

- You were awake all night. If you didn't know better, you'd think your bed had been shaking. The next morning you discover there was an earthquake where your father lives, hundreds of miles away.

- The smell of roses wafts into the room. You look around; there aren't any flowers anywhere. Several hours later, a client enters the room. She's wearing rose perfume.

- Why does your ankle seem wrenched? You're just sitting on a park bench! A stranger hops to the bench, grimacing while holding her ankle. That explains it.

- "What a handsome watch," you think, holding the timepiece found in your grandfather's jewelry box. Immediately you start experiencing different moments in his life. Every memory involves the watch: the day his father gave it to him, the evening he put it in the box before entering the service, and its shiny presence in his pocket when he married your grandmother.

As you can imagine, physical empaths fulfill incredibly important roles in the empathic universe. Physical empaths make sure that humans satisfy their obligations to nature, assuring that we tend to the environment and the beings within it. Through physical empathy we can even sense if our pets are ill or well, hurting or happy, hungry or satiated.

By sensing what is occurring with our fellow human beings, we can provide and care for each other. A parent can tell if her newborn needs a diaper change or a trip to the doctor. A physician can determine what might be wrong with a patient.

As an example, I once worked with an emergency-room doctor who frequently sensed his patients' issues in his own body. One time, when examining a patient complaining of a headache, the doctor felt his own chest tighten. He knew that there was nothing wrong with his own heart, so he ordered an electrocardiogram for the patient. The test revealed that the patient had recently undergone a heart attack. The doctor's quick thinking—and physical empathy—saved the patient's life.

Some physical empaths attune to wartime, terrorist, or other tragic events. For example, years ago I received emails from several clients who had been physically attuned to the terrorist attacks on the World Trade Center on September 11, 2001. The previous night, one client dreamed that she was in a plane crash. After the attacks, another client smelled smoke everywhere he went for weeks; few people know that the buildings smoldered for months after the tragedy. The stories went on and on.

As you might imagine, most physical empaths, especially those who most frequently experience others' discomfort and trauma in their own bodies, question the desirability of their gift. Plain and simple, it doesn't feel good to feel others' physical problems. Inherently, however, sensing others' challenges, aches, and pains is an incredible facility. When we sense horror in another person or being, we are more apt to treat them better and get others to do the same. Those who can explain the atrocities of war on the victims can instill care and compassion in their fellow humans, and maybe even prevent a catastrophe.

Physical empaths can read more than traumatizing bodily issues. They can also pick up on pleasant sensations. How wonderful for the grandmother to *really* know that her granddaughter loves a birthday present. What about that personal trainer who can feel the growing strength in a client? He can differentiate between the exercises that are working and those that aren't. Even physical objects can bestow a physical empath with impressions, doing so through a process called psychometry.

Psychometry is the ability to sense information about another person through an object, usually one that was important to the owner. For instance, I inherited a silver compact handed down from oldest daughter to oldest daughter. Every time I hold it, I can sense my various "grandmothers"—what they look like, felt like, and liked to do. Of course, this physical empathy gift is not limited to attuning to people. You could hold a dog collar and tell the dog's owner all about Fido!

For all the variations of physical empathy, the gift always involves experiencing someone or something else's physical sensations. A sampling includes the following:

Another's Bodily Discomforts

These include unpleasant problems including aches, pains, illnesses, diseases, wounds, injuries, and hunger; signs of stress, such as changes in heartbeat, blood pressure, and sleep patterns; and the causes of bodily discomforts, such as constrictive clothing, rough handling, being struck, and more.

Another's Bodily Comforts

These comprise the sensations involved when the body is being healed, stroked, touched, or relieved of pain, and also reactions to positive experiences, such as feeling nourished, sexually turned on, clothed correctly, or treated well.

Attunement to Natural Beings

The ability to sense comfort and discomfort in natural species, such as animals, fish, and reptiles; plants, trees, and flowers; and just anything else in nature. You might sense anything from the flow of water on a fish's scales to burning sensations of a tree during a wildfire.

Reactions to the Environment

This capability allows you to attune to what feels good, neutral, or dangerous in the environment, whether that environment is human-made or natural. For instance, many people and living beings are negatively impacted by artificial electromagnetic activity, as well as gruesome sounds, so you might pick up on a person's or animal's reactions to power lines or unnatural noises. You might also feel how people or natural beings react to earth changes, including hurricanes, storms, droughts, solar flares, and more. As well, you might possibly sense the energy in a room and perceive how it affects others. For instance, if a room is so small that a friend feels claustrophobic, you might attune to her sense of being smothered and compressed.

Energies Stored in Objects

Strong electromagnetic activity and sound can be held in physical objects. I'll share a science study in the next section underscoring this point. How might you experience this occurrence? Imagine that you were wearing a certain ring when you met your best friend. Every time you wear the ring again, you recall how you were clothed, how you stood, and what your body felt like during that first meeting. Echoes can be held within all kinds of objects, from jewelry to furniture.

As you might expect, physical empathy can present an array of challenges, which are also important to know about. They include the following:

Physical Overempathy

As a physical empath, you can potentially come down with illnesses, aches, pains, and signs of stress that aren't your own. You might also become confused about your true state of healthiness. For instance, pretend that a friend is at a healthy weight and you are overweight. By overidentifying with your friend's state of fitness, you might ignore the fact that *you* should be dieting.

Taking On the Woes of the World

For you, the traumas caused by climate change, war, genocide, and other dramas might be all too real. As already suggested in this chapter, overempaths are also likely to be highly sensitive to electromagnetic and sound pollution and alterations in cosmic and earthly energies, such as solar rays, moons and tides, and volcanic eruptions.

Physical Underempathy

Underempaths often fail to sense or pick up on others' reactions to life events and bodily needs. Some underempaths are born that way. Others are simply untrained or might have been so open empathically that they closed down to protect themselves. Being underempathic carries a high cost. You might fail to pick up on dangers that could harm you, whether caused by the environment, an animal, or a person. You might have difficulties making or keeping friends since you can't relate to their most primal and physical experiences.

Physical Empathic Manipulation

Some physical empaths, including narcissists, can famously (or infamously) attune to the physical problems and needs of others, but not for reasons of sharing compassion; rather, they use this data to their personal advantage, perhaps as fodder for coercion or bribery. For instance, picture a narcissistic mom who wants to force her young son to do the cleaning for her. Upon sensing his hunger, she could refuse to feed him unless he cleans the house. A different narcissist might tune in to a subject's physical pain or ailment and embarrass them until the victim snaps to the narcissist's marching orders. I've even seen narcissists twist another person's sense of bodily pleasure to their advantage, such as by attuning to a partner's sexual desires. Having seduced a victim, the narcissist then refuses to meet their sexual needs unless they are given what they want. Of course, it's just as likely that a physical empath finds themselves at the other end of the empathic manipulation, resonating so completely to another's physical desires, needs, and issues that they fail to care for themselves.

How do you know if you're being manipulated? You're being deceived if you're being harmed while the other is being helped. For instance, imagine that you find yourself paying all the bills because your partner has so much pain that it's hard (but not impossible) for them to work. Are they really too achy to pick up the house, wash their own dishes, and put away the laundry? Not really. The strong physical empathic must guard all aspects of their physicality, from sexuality to the expenditure of money.

You'll be assisted with looking for the reasons you might be over- or underempathic or involved in manipulation in exercise 6, "Deprogramming Your Physical Empathy," featured later in this chapter. In general, physical empathy usually goes awry during childhood. For instance, if a child's own physical wishes and needs were only met if they physically tended to a family member or took on others' physical illnesses and pains, they are likely to continue this pattern with others after growing up. For instance, in my family I took on everyone's physical issues; that was my way of loving them. When I attended therapy and figured out that most of my allergies didn't belong to me, they disappeared—and within days most of them appeared in my family members.

Manipulative tendencies, which involve being manipulative or manipulated, often occur because of unmet childhood needs. Narcissism begins in infancy, when we're supposed to be the sole focus of a caretaker. When this doesn't happen, a child learns that they will only get their needs met if they figure out what a parent is physically experiencing. "Dad is drunk," observes a child. "Now I can get him to buy me something." In adulthood, that same child might continue reading others' physical realities to trick them into focusing on them.

Children are susceptible to being manipulated if the conditions of being loved or surviving depend on knowing what another is physically experiencing. For instance, maybe a child observes that if they're nice to mommy when she's sick, they will get attention; otherwise, they are ignored. Guess what? That child will grow up and partner with a mate who is constantly unhappy and ill. Inadvertently, the manipulative adult that models (or benefits from) this type of patterning is using their child's physical empathy to avoid their own responsibilities.

Some physical empaths grew up in a family in which no one modeled physical empathy. If you were hungry, sick, or in pain, you were ignored. This can be a sure setup for becoming empathically shut down or manipulative. But there are also positive reasons to be a physical empath. Perhaps you experienced the benefits of caring for others by relating to them in a past life. Maybe you have a healer's soul; you are here to sense others' physical needs so you can assist them. Someone whose life purpose involves tending to animals, gardens, or the environment is heartily benefited by their physical empathy skills. Inherently, physical empathy is a good thing. Especially when the tendency to be empathically manipulative derives from childhood environment, such as through neglect or trauma, the choice to learn and change can alter negative patterns. Even if the inclination is genetic, we're all educable and deserve to benefit from our empathic abilities.

The Mechanics of Physical Empathy
How It All Makes Sense

As discussed in chapter 1, empathy is managed by a combination of physical and subtle-energy interactions. Basically, our nervous system attunes to what another is going through and registers, if not deeply mirrors, what is happening within them. We also garner energy, both physical and subtle, through our energetic fields, such as our electromagnetic fields and the auric fields. What enters and is rejected is a matter of our empathic boundaries.

Probably more than any other of the four total empathic styles, our physical empathy boundaries are programmed by our genes, ancestral experiences, and the environment in which we're raised or are living. In other words, physical reality creates our physical empathic boundaries.

In a nutshell, genes are the codes that determine physical traits such as eye and hair color. But they also impact our empathic ability. For instance, they decide how many motor neurons we'll have and how easy it will be to access them. Case in point, we've talked about how hard it is for people with autism and psychopathy to be empathic. Overall, genes affect about 10 percent of everyone's core empathic ability (Sandoiu 2018).

Even more interesting are specific types of genes and how they directly (and strangely) impact physical empathy. These are epigenes, and they are the subject of epigenetics, the study of how our ancestors' memories affect us. Epigenes, a biological soup that surrounds our regular DNA, stores our ancestors' recollections, including the short- and long-term effects of the environment, illness, tragedies, violence, and pleasant times. I believe that a physically empathic gift or experience becomes obvious when a real-life event or the story from an empathic subject triggers related epigenetic material.

For instance, imagine that your great-grandmother went through a horrific famine, during which time food was scarce. Her reactions are loaded into your epigenes. Now fancy that you're talking to a person who survived a drought. Suddenly, your stomach clenches. You feel starved and light-headed. Your muscles become weak and you picture yourself as skin and bones. It's logical to surmise that your physical empathy is intensified because the chemicals related to your great-grandmother's experiences, which match the drought victim's, are triggered and flood your system.

It's also possible that your physical empathy, or a physically empathic event, can relate to past-life experiences.

Many healers and cultures believe in reincarnation; I do too. Keeping the former example in mind, imagine that you starved to death in a previous lifetime. Memories of past-life events are transferred into the body at birth through the soul. Your empathic relation to a deprivation victim might hit you intensely because you've been through a similar situation, albeit eras ago.

As already shared, some physical empaths also attune to beings and events in the natural world, as well as fluctuations in geomagnetic and solar activity. Science underscores the fact we've a built-in apparatus for the latter sensitivity. In fact, research shows that the heartbeat, breathing, and digestive system of most individuals actually respond almost immediately to alterations in cosmic radiation and solar winds (Heartmath Institute 2018).

As an explanation for how we share physically empathic data, science is proving that physical sensations can actually transfer from one being to another. Interestingly, this transmission can even occur through tangible materials. One incredible research project, conducted by the Oregon Health and Science University, verified the ease with which physical sensations like pain can transfer. Overall, the study showed that not only did observing mice demonstrate the same physical symptoms revealed by a single mouse in pain, but they would also show pain when affected by the bedding of mice that had been hurt (McDonald 2016).

As this study suggests, pain transfers. As physical empaths know, so does pleasure—and not only from person to person or living being to living being, but even through objects. It's pretty clear that this ability exists and with the correct training, we can apply it.

Indications of Physical Empathy
The Good, the Bad, and the Ugly

You've probably already figured out several ways that a subject sending physical empathy data can knock on your door. Think physical empathy if you sense any of the following:

- aches, pains, and other sensations that aren't comfortable

- sensations of inflammation, heaviness, or congestion

- tingling, itching, and bubbling sensations

- sense of being ill or sick; also exhibition of illness symptoms

- numbness or lack of bodily awareness

- smells, aromas, the sense of being touched or of tasting, and other sensory indications that don't apply to you or seem logical
- bodily awareness, real-life memories, echoes of the past arising from an object
- cessation of your ability to control a part or the entirety of your body
- relating to the physical activities or movements made by other people or natural beings
- relating to the physical traumas of a group of people, individuals, or the same in relation to natural beings, such as when (or before or after) they experience war, violence, climactic catastrophe, or the like
- awareness of what is happening in others as related to their relationship with the physical world, such as their homes, the natural world, finances, and other basic needs
- sensitivity to occurrences in nature, natural beings, natural objects, or events caused by subtle or physical forces, such as radiation, solar flares, and digital information

As a special note, I want to expand on my very last point. The world is becoming increasingly digitalized. Can you imagine how many gazillion bits of information are constantly bombarding you, even when you're sleeping? Yes, all of that internet-conveyed information, exchanged emails, and transferred television and cable information is flying around. A physical empath is often highly reactive to this data, even if they aren't aware of it.

For instance, I worked with a little boy who could hardly ever sleep. Every so often he'd just drop, too exhausted to keep going. This could occur at school or even on the playground but became worse anytime he was around a computer or modem. His mother was greatly concerned and brought him to see me.

I perceived him to be such a high physical empath that he was absorbing nearly all the digital data flitting around. I walked him through a version of exercise 6, "Deprogramming Your Physical Empathy," to discover that he unconsciously thought that collecting data would keep him safe. We shifted his programs, a concept we'll explain the the next section, and he immediately started sleeping normally.

Are you ready to examine your own physical empathic boundaries and gifts? Then let's get started.

• EXERCISE 6 •

Deprogramming Your Physical Empathy

The term "programs" refers to the beliefs that run your system and consequently your physical and subtle behavior. It can be important to figure out which programs are in charge of your physical empathy and to assess if they are working for or against you, especially if your physical empathy isn't bolstering your life or if you want to squeeze even more benefits from it. This is because overall, healthy programs will enable supportive empathic boundaries and unhealthy programs will cause underempathy, overempathy, or the strains of manipulation. This exercise is designed to help you uncover, rewrite, and adjust your physical empathy programs so that all your empathic boundaries are wholesome.

One aspect of this exercise is the introduction to the color pink. It's a lifesaver in its ability to cleanse, renew, and establish strong physical boundaries. Pink is composed of red and white. Red represents power, passion, and physical vitality. White provides spirituality, integrity, and purity. Together, these two colors invite your spirit to decide exactly who or what is advantageous to physically relate to.

You can return to this exercise at any time. Our issues are multi-layered and can also be situation specific, which means that we often have to dig deeper—or repetitively—to deal with arising physical empathy issues.

STEP ONE: **Prepare.** Settle into a comfortable space and make sure you won't be disturbed for a few minutes. If you feel most comfortable with music, incense, or some other type of sensory support, use them to create ambience. Also gather writing equipment to keep track of what you discover through this process.

STEP TWO: **Conduct Spirit-to-Spirit.** Affirm your spirit, all the helping spirits—including any linked to the people or situations that programmed your physical empathic boundaries—and the Spirit. Now turn the process over to the Spirit.

STEP THREE: **Remember a Positive.** Recall a situation in which you were physically empathic and felt great about the process and the outcome. Obtain a psychic image, message, or bodily sense that explains the causes of the uplifting programs, which originated in any of the following time periods:

- *Past lives:* Did you learn an important physical empathy lesson during a past life? See if a situation comes to mind.

- *Epigenetics:* Maybe an ancestor was gifted in physical empathy. This often occurs amongst healers, physicians, herbalists, farmers, astrologers, and the like. Is an ancestor's experience informing you?

- *Family of origin:* Was your childhood family particularly respectful of physical boundaries and empathic insights? If so, they did you a favor. What did they do right?

- *Personal experiences:* As life moves forward, we often obtain the types of inspiration and skills that forge decent empathic boundaries. See if events related to this category pop into your mind.

Now condense your musings into a single sentence that encapsulates your baseline positive program. For example, you might write, "I have learned to allow the Spirit to make all decisions regarding my physical empathy."

STEP FOUR: **Recall a Negative.** Next, think about a circumstance in which you employed physical empathy and were either over- or underempathic or stuck in a manipulative loop. Ask the Spirit for a psychic image, message, or bodily message to highlight the causes of the damaging programs, which could have been initiated in any or all of these time periods:

- *Past lives:* Are there past-life experiences that created an empathic wound? Spend as much time as needed to let feelings, images, and memories of applicable situations formulate in your mind.

- *Epigenetics:* Sometimes ancestral experiences establish conditions that distort our empathic boundaries. Ask the Spirit if you can picture or relate to applicable ancestors' challenges. You might even recall a pertinent family story.

- *Family of origin:* Was your childhood family particularly disrespectful in relation to physical boundaries? Did you have to consciously or unconsciously adapt to the family system in a way that caused empathic harm? See what situations arise within you.

- *Personal experiences:* Our own experiences might have created negative empathic boundaries. Relate to whatever you have gone through.

Now summarize your assessment into a single sentence that describes your physical empathy weakness. For instance, you might say, "I believe that I must take on everyone's illnesses to be loved."

STEP FIVE: **Forge a New Program.** Keep in mind the positive and negative statements that you've formulated in regard to your physical empathy. Now ask the Spirit to assist you in developing a healthy replacement belief. It will incorporate your healthy programming and transform the negative one. For instance, I might knit the statements I already presented in this way:

"I am so worthy of love that I allow the Spirit to make all decisions about my physical empathy, even if others don't approve of the outcome."

STEP SIX: **Cleanse and Renew.** It's time to clear away the negative programs causing unhealthy empathic boundaries and to anchor the fresh program. Ask the Spirit to beam healing streams through all aspects of you across time. These streams will wash you of all detrimental energies in a safe and gentle way. Then ask the Spirit to pour any needed shades of pink through you. This color will revitalize your physical and subtle bodies and align your empathic boundaries according to the Spirit's will.

STEP SEVEN: **Close.** When you feel restored, thank the Spirit and all spirits concerned for the illuminating information and vital transformation, then return to your everyday life.

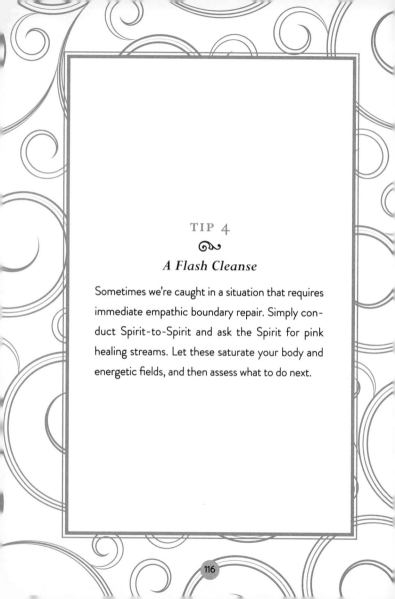

TIP 4

ॐ

A Flash Cleanse

Sometimes we're caught in a situation that requires immediate empathic boundary repair. Simply conduct Spirit-to-Spirit and ask the Spirit for pink healing streams. Let these saturate your body and energetic fields, and then assess what to do next.

• EXERCISE 7 •

Analyzing a Physically Empathic Message

How do you assess the meaning of a physically received empathic message? Equally important, how do you separate incoming information from your own bodily sensations? This exercise can be used to perform both maneuvers when relating to a living being or even a group of beings. In the latter case, simply treat the group consciousness as a single entity.

This exercise is styled to be used at two different times, which are right after you've received a possible physically based empathic communication or long after you obtained empathic information. I'll walk you through the steps as if you're analyzing an on-the-spot message.

STEP ONE: **Become Aware.** As explained in the section "Indications of Physical Empathy" on page 107, there are many indicators of a physically empathic message. All involve bodily awareness. Without judging the message, its sender, or its meaning, accept that you might be receiving an empathic communiqué.

STEP TWO: **Conduct Spirit-to-Spirit.** Affirm your spirit, the spirit or spirits sending the empathic message, all helping spirits, and the Spirit.

STEP THREE: **Interact with the Message.** Ask the Spirit to apply healing streams to adjust your empathic boundaries for the incoming message. These streams will do whatever is required, which could include any of the following:

- turn off a message not meant for you or not good for you
- lessen the flow of data
- increase the flow of energy
- direct the energy appropriately within your body so it registers and isn't stored

If the current turns off, ask the Spirit to cleanse and release you from the process, fully restored, and also assist anyone else involved. Then release yourself from the process. If you continue to receive data, ask the Spirit to provide you beneficial insights, as applicable, pertaining to the following areas of interest.

- *Source of the data:* From who or what is this information coming? If you don't need to know, you'll sense the Spirit's ambivalence. It's okay to not always know a source; simply continue with this process. Otherwise, accept the answer you receive, which might come as a knowing, a vision, an internal voice, or already be obvious.

- *What should I understand about the message:* Pause until you thoroughly comprehend what you're supposed to know. Is there a physical trauma, problem, opportunity, or some other situation facing the subject? Are there particulars that you need to understand? Are you simply supposed to sense what is occurring with the subject? Ask any other question that pops into your mind.

- *What should I do about the message:* Is there something to say, do, or know in reaction to the empathic message?

Do you need to internally or physically mirror the subject, as you were shown how to do in exercise 5? Ask the Spirit for input and trust your gut or another psychic response. Then take action if you are supposed to.

- *Permit the Spirit to operate:* As you have discovered, this exercise helps you relate to the Spirit more than the empathic sender. This is for your protection and allows for perfect action. Ask the Spirit to simply do what else needs to be done.

STEP FOUR: **Cleanse Yourself and Others.** When finished, ask the Spirit to employ healing streams to cleanse and restore all involved in this interaction.

STEP FIVE: **Close.** When you feel safe and energetically filled up, return to your normal life, acknowledging that the Spirit will continue to help everyone requiring assistance.

TIP 5

❧

Empathizing Physically
with an Animal

You can employ exercise 7, "Analyzing a Physically Empathic Message," to physically empathize with an animal. To gain the most information, stretch your boundaries a bit. An animal's senses—seeing, hearing, and feeling—extend beyond a human's senses. While relating to the animal, ask the Spirit to better enhance your own senses so you can truly understand what the animal is going through on the physical level. Then, when closing, ask the Spirit to readjust your boundaries for normal human functioning.

TIP 6

ⴲ

*Relating Physically
to a Part of Yourself*

What if you are relating to a part of yourself, such as a wounded inner child or a past-life self? It's easy to do. Simply walk through the same steps outlined in exercise 7, but transform the needy part of yourself into the subject. Request that the Spirit surround this self with healing streams to keep it separate from your everyday self so you can communicate with it. Then conduct the exercise. When closing, ask the Spirit to dissolve these streams and gently reintegrate this part of yourself into your current self.

Empathically Reading an
Object with Psychometry

As explained, many physical empaths can attune to the subtle energy contained within an object. Not every object holds legible, or readable, information. The easiest to read are talismans, jewelry, paintings, furniture, or similar objects that have been important to a person or a family. Other common data holders are gemstones and other oft-used elemental objects. Even the water in a lake that is frequently enjoyed by individuals or living beings can convey information.

In order to enable you to enjoy and apply this type of physical empathy, I'm going to help you decipher the energy hold within a single object—specifically, one that has been special to its owner. You can use the same technique for nearly anything after you're familiar with the process. Know, however, that some objects don't hold energy. If during step four you don't sense any incoming energy, simply ask for healing streams to renew you and close down before exiting the process.

STEP ONE: **Prepare.** Find an object that has been well-used, perhaps quite loved, and holds sentimental value to its owner. Sit near or hold this object.

STEP TWO: **Conduct Spirit-to-Spirit.** Affirm your spirit, the spirits of the person or people affiliated with the object, any helping spirits, and the Spirit. Then take a few deep breaths.

STEP THREE: **Connect with the Object.** Think about the object's owner and then request that the Spirit use healing streams to link you with the object in a safe way.

STEP FOUR: **Bring In the Information.** Request that the Spirit next employ these streams to bring energy from the object into you. These energies will safely infuse your system and allow your body to relate to its owner, specifically attuning you to a specific experience or set of experiences in the owner's life that are linked to the object.

The events recorded in the object will replay within your bodily self. You might become aware of what the owner was wearing, thinking, feeling, and even seeing during a specific experience or set of events. You might feel as if you are walking in their shoes as per internal mirroring. As the memories pour into you, ask the Spirit to reveal what made this object so important to the owner. What was its role or innate value? The relationship between the owner and the object? Continue until you feel satiated.

STEP FIVE: **Ask to Assist.** We can always use our physical empathy to improve a situation, even if the person requiring assistance is long passed or separated by distance. Ask the Spirit if there is a prayer or blessing you need to formulate for the object's owner. Then ask the Spirit to send this loving energy to the owner's or subject's soul through the object. Objects are two-way doorways. They can send information to you but also from you. Allow all that needs to happen to transpire.

STEP SIX: **Release Yourself.** Request that the Spirit uses healing streams to easily and gently release you from the energies in the object and owner. Know that the Spirit will affix everything and everyone in their right place.

STEP SEVEN: **Close.** When you feel complete, take a few deep breaths. Thank the spirit of the owner and the Spirit for allowing you this private communion, and continue with your life.

Physical Is as Physical Does

If you are a strong physical empath, your body can benefit from physical activities to rebalance itself after an empathic experience. I'm an extreme physical empath and have found that the following activities nourish and reenergize me.

Take an Epsom Salt Bath

Epsom salts are famous among esoterics and empaths for recalibrating the nervous system and pulling others' energies, as well as negative forces like solar winds, out of the body. Follow the directions on the package and let yourself linger in the water for as long as possible. I also recommend that you add a drop or two of the following essential oils to the water, as long as you aren't allergic to them:

LAVENDER: Calms and soothes. Frees you from others' frenetic or disturbed energies.

ROSE: Releases the energies of those you are concerned about. Very useful if you continue to sense or think about a subject's physical condition and feel powerless to help.

EUCALYPTUS: Useful if you hold on to another's physical discomfort, including bruising, pain, and achiness.

FRANKINCENSE: This mystically charged oil connects you and those you were empathizing with to the holiest of spirits, which can free you of unnecessary energies.

Essential Oils

To support healthy empathic boundaries, you can also use the just-listed essential oils topically, usually by mixing a drop or two in a carrier oil such as almond oil, and also through aromatherapy. Follow the directions given on the oil packages or aromatherapy dispensers.

Gemstones and Other Rocks

There are specific stones that are useful for the physical empath. While you are performing any of the exercises offered in this chapter, you can hold one, put it in a pocket, or use it as jewelry. Many physical empaths also fill their houses with gemstones or rocks in order to sustain their empathic boundaries and filter out unwanted data. If you use a stone frequently, cleanse it by setting it outside in the sunlight, moonlight, or rain for twenty-four hours or by putting it in a glass jar that contains a tablespoon of Epsom salts and enough water to cover the stone completely. You can shake the jar for a few minutes and then set it outside for twenty-four hours. Then empty the container and use the stone again whenever you desire.

For the purpose of physical empathy, I recommend the following stones:

MOUNTAIN ROCKS: Limestone, shale, and other mountain rocks are very grounding and will help you separate from others' energies.

HERKIMER DIAMOND: When these quartz crystals are contained in the dark volcanic stone that surrounds them, they cleanse you and others of negative energy and ground all concerned in everyday reality.

AGATES: Agates separate your body and physical energies from the same in others.

GARNETS AND RUBIES: These bright red stones ignite your personal life energy and keep you nourished during and after a physical empathy interaction.

Pink Flannel

What if you are adversely affected by the negativity of technology? Maybe you are EMF sensitive or feel traumatized after watching a violent scene on the news. Pink flannel absorbs negative electromagnetic activity and can help transform those energies into neutral or helpful energies. You can put a strip of pink flannel under a computer or over the top of a television, paste a piece on your phone, or sit on a square of flannel if you're using technology.

I believe pink flannel is protective for two main reasons. Flannel absorbs and can therefore soak up EMF. Pink is a combination of white, which establishes spiritual parameters, and red, which takes in vital energies such as electricity. Add the flannel to your regular laundry every week or so to free it from collected energies.

Amber Eyeglasses

Physical empaths are often negatively affected by the blue light emitted from computers, smartphones, game consoles, and similar technologies. Amber- or yellow-tinted eyeglasses block the blue light and alleviate both eye strain and brain overstimulation, also reducing your susceptibility to picking up empathic data you don't want. You can easily purchase these glasses over the internet.

Get in the Dirt

Physical empaths must nourish their bodies with lots of outdoor activities. Better yet, perform earthing, which involves walking with bare feet in the soil, sand, grass, or other earth elements.

Supportive Foods

Our physical empathic abilities strain certain physical organs, including the kidneys and adrenals. Following a heavy-duty physical empathy interaction, or if you're an often-stimulated physical empath, make sure you eat a lot of clean proteins, such as grass-fed meat or the equivalent in the vegan category. Also enjoy plenty of green vegetables and drink a lot of water.

Now that you've acquainted with your physical empathy, it's time to turn the corner and get emotional.

Chapter Four

EMOTIONAL EMPATHY
The Instrument for Feelings

Have you ever felt another's feelings as if they were your own—and maybe even become confused because you just can't figure it out? Are *you* angry—or does the anger belong to your friend, mom, dog, or that stranger on the television? Are you aware of your own love-based need or is someone else sending out a message?

Emotional empathy is the ability to understand another's feelings. An innate drive, it enables bonding, relating, and compassion. If another's feelings replace or cover up our own, however, we can fall prey to codependency and other challenges. Conversely, if we can't connect to another's emotional narrative, we can become very lonely indeed.

I'll begin this chapter by sharing illustrations of emotional empathy, showcasing the many facets of this gift. I'll then probe the science explaining emotional empathy and the various ways that it can appear, along with the positive and negative effects of this mystical aptitude. And then I'll present a variety of techniques and tips that will make good—and safe—use of your emotional empathy.

Feeling Another's Feelings

We've all experienced some level of emotional empathy, or the ability to feel another's feelings. Like a multifaceted diamond, however, emotional empathy has many facets. As the following examples will prove, there are many ways to be emotionally sensitive.

Imagine yourself in settings like the following:

- You wonder why your friend can't tell that her dog, Katie, is sad. Petal, their other pet dog, just died. You can tell that Katie is really missing Petal, but your friend seems clueless.

- Your friend sits across from you. Despite the fact that she's smiling, your insides insist that she's angry.

- You've always had test anxiety. Then one day, you realized that you were absorbing everyone else's fears and feeling them in addition to your own.

- Sometimes you don't even want to go to the movies. No matter what a character feels, you are right there, whether angry, sad, embarrassed, or happy.

- You don't like crowds. It seems that too many groups reduce to a sort of "group feeling," a hysterical, singular emotion.

Emotional empathy is the core of personal bonding. The ability to sense another's emotions within our own body enables them to feel understood and loved. In turn, we feel closer to them. And then, depending on what someone is feeling, we can adjust our words and behavior. As well, if we've hurt someone's feelings, we can right a wrong.

Emotional empathy also enables communal bonding and progress. Because people are more similar than not, we can compose laws that promote the welfare of all. Emotional empathy can also encourage us to enforce those rules and act morally. We're more apt to respect others if we can sense how mistreatment affects them. Furthermore, lack of emotional empathy is one of the main reasons that people hurt each other.

Logically, it's far easier to discriminate against someone because of race, gender, religion, or sexual preference if we don't understand how horrible it feels to be discriminated against. In the same vein, emotional empathy can catalyze social change. Recently I read a news article that described the hardships of young male Syrian teenage refugees in Greece. I was so appalled that I wrote the article's photographer to see if there was anything I could do. He wrote back and suggested that I contribute to an organization that was making a difference; I did.

Emotional empathy can also keep us safe. Manipulators, for instance, fake their emotions. They might be angry but act concerned. If we can trust our emotional gut, we won't fall for the surface presentation.

As an example, I once worked with a client who never felt cared about by his wife, even though she did all the right things. Her eyes would tear up when he was sad. She'd stroke his arm when he needed comfort.

She'd break out the wine to celebrate his achievements. I tested the situation out when they were both in my office together.

I began the session by asking him to share two events, first a disturbing one and then a fulfilling one. She was to respond to his disclosures and I would then offer my sense of what was transpiring emotionally between them.

The husband started by reviewing the events around his father's recent death. When he wept, his wife held his hand. I felt chilled, however, like she was actually cold, not warm, on the inside. The husband then laughed while describing the antics of their new puppy. She smiled, but to me, her emotions seemed tight and angry. The husband was relieved that I had sensed the distinction. The wife wasn't pleased, but she was willing to figure out what was truly happening inside of her. Basically, she'd never received attention growing up, causing her to be jealous of anything, negative or positive, that took her husband's attention.

I recommended that the wife work with a therapist to recall and express the various feelings she had repressed since childhood. She did. She and her husband then returned for a joint session after about a year. She was a different person. She was simultaneously calm and bubbly and interacted lovingly with her husband. Both of them were able to share their feelings and be heard by each other. I've found that emotional manipulators or the empathy-challenged in general usually were neglected as children or had to use their empathic abilities in a twisted way in order to survive. If we weren't treated as important when growing up or as an adult, we deserve to reclaim the right to our personal needs, feelings, and thoughts. No one can fully care for another until they can fully care about themselves.

Humans aren't the only species that feel feelings. As I'll explain in the next section, there are biochemical and electromagnetic pathways for receiving, feeling, and sending emotions in animals and other natural beings, including plants and trees. Depending on our capability, we can relate to feelings from just about any animate being—and, as we'll discuss in chapter 6, any spiritual being as well.

What types of emotional knowledge can you pick up from others? How might you sense an emotionally empathic moment? Here are several possibilities.

Another's Emotional Stressors

Certain emotions indicate that the subject is stressed. These are often called "negative emotions" and include anger, sadness, fear, disgust, rage, guilt, shame, jealousy, envy, despair, and hopelessness. These feelings and others like them, such as intense grief and powerlessness, are all parts of the five basic feeling constellations and call for change. I'll describe some of the negative emotions associated with the five core feeling categories in the following list, each of which requests specific and outlined responses:

ANGER: Includes rage, hatred, jealousy, and anger. Indicates that you must set a boundary.

SADNESS: Includes deep grief, despair, hopelessness, and feeling lost. Suggests that it is time to seek more deeply for love or go somewhere else for it.

FEAR: Includes terror, abandonment, panic, and powerlessness. Insists that you look for a more secure place or try a safer behavior.

DISGUST: Includes shame, blame, guilt, embarrassment, and shyness. Suggests you must release the lie of being unworthy or undeserving.

Another's Celebratory Emotions

The so-called positive emotions are all versions of joy, the first major type of feeling. Specific versions indicate the following needs:

HAPPINESS: Remain in the moment; do more of what's being done

SATISFACTION: Accept and revel in the state of fullness

BLISS: Acknowledge and enjoy the connection

GRATITUDE: Accept grace

FORGIVENESS: Release the blockage to love

Another's Emotional Needs

Sometimes we don't perceive another's actual feelings. Instead, we attune to an emotional need, picking up that they need a hug, smile, word of advice, friend, or our quiet presence. This awareness leads to what is called "emotional compassion," or the ability to emotionally attend to another.

A Group's Emotional Consciousness

Sometimes, the feelings of the individuals in a group blend and turn into a singular and huge wave of emotional energy. The process involved is called "emotional contagion," and I'll further discuss it in the next section, "The Mechanics of Emotional Empathy." When the group emotion is positive, such as amongst a group of spiritual masters who focus on love, uplifting and bonding experiences can follow. If the group emotion is detrimental, such as what occurred when Hitler motivated a nation to hate the Jews, catastrophe can occur. People can override their own morals and sense of rightness.

Attunement to Natural Beings

As you'll discover in the next section, most living beings have at least a rudimentary network for emotional attunement. We can potentially resonate with the feelings of all natural species, including animals, reptiles, insects, arthropods, fish, amphibians, rodents, and the like, as well as trees, flowers, and other plants. Certain people can also relate to the feelings of the earth and other planets, as well as the stars. I have clients who swear they can feel the groaning of the earth in a highly polluted area or the plight of a star or planet under a meteoroid siege.

Emotional Sensations in the Environment

An atmosphere can brim with emotional charges, which can linger after emotions have been expressed by an individual or created through an exchange between beings. For example, after a heated argument, anger often lingers in a room—but so can joy and other emotions.

As you might expect, emotional empathy can create any number of problems, which I'll next describe.

Emotional Overempathy

Overempaths are so spongy that others' emotions often get stuck in their own body. This is because most overempaths have too-porous empathic boundaries, which don't deflect another's emotions or release them after they've been analyzed. Quite typically, the alien feelings overpower the overempath's emotions, causing scenarios and conditions that can be difficult to diagnose and change. After all, we can't process feelings that don't belong to us.

How might we be affected by another's internalized emotions? I once worked with a client who erupted in rage for no known reason. He had been treated with prescription medications and was undergoing talk therapy. The rage attacks only disappeared when he figured out that he was expressing his father's rage, which he had absorbed at an early age in order to create more peace in the family. If you have this tendency, you'll learn how to address it through several exercises in this chapter.

Emotional Underempathy

Underempaths aren't able to respond to others' emotions or emotional needs, which can lead to lack of bonding and the sense of being unlovable. While some underempaths are biologically challenged, there is evidence that it's possible to teach emotional empathy. Other underempaths close down because it was too hard to process or react to the level of chaos in their family system. Still others were deficient in empathic models. Emotional connectivity is core to developing genuine relationships, which means it's important to activate emotional empathy or learn how to develop it, one of the purposes of this chapter.

Emotional Empathic Manipulation

There are two sides to emotional manipulation. Manipulators often access others' emotions and use them to their advantage. For example, I had a client whose psychopathic father would act like he understood his feelings. After he was nice, he'd turn around and "borrow" money from my client—and never pay it back. Those manipulated emotionally often put up with abuse, as did my client, to get a grain of love and attention. And as my client said, "I don't want to hurt my dad's feelings just because he hurts mine." That's called codependency, the act of helping others, only to be injured ourselves.

You'll uncover the reasons you might be over- or underempathic or involved in manipulation in exercise 9, "Deprogramming Your Emotional Empathy." Suffice it to say that most of the situations that distort our emotional boundaries are rooted in childhood. It's nearly impossible to sense others' emotions if no one responded to our own. On the other hand, at least one of the children within a dysfunctional family is often raised to be the "heart," or emotional sponge. It's their job to alleviate the family friction and disorders by carrying—and caring for—what everyone else is going through.

Many discriminatory attitudes and "isms," such as racism and sexism, are actually forms of emotional contagion. I worked with a client who grew up in a racist family that belonged to the KKK. He hated his family's prejudice and was the only one to escape the toxic philosophy. He eventually became a therapist and figured out that his family was infected with an intense fear of people different than themselves, which led to their hatred. Unfortunately, it's hard to escape this type of emotional contagion if we believe we'll lose our identity by doing so.

The Mechanics of Emotional Empathy

Emotional empathy is the primary type of empathy for forming bonds. I sometimes call it relational empathy, as its main purpose is to connect us with others. Its benefits are measurable; in fact, one study shows that 90 percent of the top performers in the workplace have a high emotional intelligence in that they are able to sense the feelings and emotional needs of others. Emotional empathy leads to more openness and trust when relating. Comparatively, people lacking in emotional empathy are more prone to criminal behaviors, including drug dealing, thievery, and murder (Schmitz 2016).

The importance of emotional empathy is even being recognized by the medical community, which has coined the term "clinical empathy." Physicians trained in clinical empathy are better able to understand their patients' emotions. This communication is improving diagnoses and building patient-doctor trust. It also buffers doctors against burnout (Killam 2014).

As do all empathic styles, emotional empathy employs mirror neurons and the exchange of information between fields. There is one particular part of the brain that needs to be active if we're to avoid the pitfalls of emotional empathy, however, which include the inability to differentiate our emotions from others' emotions and the tendency to project our emotions upon others. It's called the supramarginal gyrus, and it overrides our natural selfishness and egocentrism (Bergland 2013).

Why is it so important to separate from others' emotions and not project our own feelings upon others? Emotional merging leads to codependency as well as emotional contagion, an activity mentioned in the last section. It's all too easy to get caught up in a "cause" or a group consciousness, leading to loss of individuality or self-degrading actions. It's not always easy to separate from a group emotion once snared by it, either. I once worked with a woman who had married into a Mafia family. After a decade, she was ready to commit suicide. Every time the Mob members did something cruel, she could feel the emotional pain of the people wronged by the mob. But the group code insisted that the family was number one, even if the family survival meant inflicting harm on the innocent. My client was clearly overempathizing with the group energy and even others' emotional issues. Rather than break away, she contemplated killing herself.

Emotional projection is destructive in particular because it messes up our ability to understand others. Imagine that you love receiving chocolate for Valentine's Day. Because of this, you give chocolate to a friend for Valentine's Day. That's okay—except that she lost her father on Valentine's Day. If you can separate your emotional opinion from hers, next year you'll give her compassion instead of chocolates. If you stubbornly hold on to your emotional opinion and continue doling out chocolates, you could injure the friendship.

One of the more exciting developments in the empathy field is research showing that animals and plants, among other living beings, are emotionally empathic. You've probably already experienced an emotionally empathic pet. In my household, every time my youngest son is ill or sad, Lucky the Lab incessantly licks his face, an obvious attempt to make it "all better." But emotional empathy stretches across all species lines, showing that nearly every type of living being is equipped with empathic neurological and electromagnetic structures. Even primitive species, including mice and rats, reveal affective or emotionally empathic behavior. In fact, some living beings, such as dolphins, have bigger emotional brain centers than humans do (Phys.org 2011).

Plants also have the sensory structures required for emotional empathy. Researchers in the relatively new field of plant neurobiology have shown that plants have communication systems comparable to those in people, minus the brain. Plants can gather information and make intelligent decisions with it, receive and send electrical signals, and even produce neurotransmitters, such as dopamine and serotonin, which enable empathic responses. They also hold memories and can learn from experience (Science Friday 2014). In fact, some researchers are starting to believe that plants are even more emotionally sensitive than animals and are able to detect twenty different physical and chemical signals, including gravity, light, magnetic field pathogens, and more (Ripper 2017).

As you can see, we can all perform emotional empathy, even animals and plants. It's important to hone and fine-tune our abilities, however, so we don't fall into the potential problems related to emotional empathy. The rest of the chapter is devoted to this empathic development.

• EXERCISE 9 •

Deprogramming Your Emotional Empathy

We want our emotional empathy to be fail-safe. To accomplish this goal, it's important to free ourselves from programs that distort our emotional boundaries and then establish solid ones. This exercise is designed to help you accomplish these tasks and can be revisited anytime.

In this exercise you'll use the color orange. Orange cleans and stabilizes emotions while balancing the neurotransmitters that manage emotions.

STEP ONE: **Prepare.** Isolate yourself in a comfortable setting and make sure you'll be left alone for a few minutes. Gather writing equipment. If desirable, light candles or use incense.

STEP TWO: **Conduct Spirit-to-Spirit.** Affirm your spirit, all the helping spirits, and any people or situations that programmed your emotional empathic boundaries. Finally, acknowledge the Spirit and turn this process over to it.

STEP THREE: **Remember a Positive.** Let arise the memory of an event in which you used your emotional empathy in a healthy fashion. You might perceive an intuitive image, recall a conversation, or remember emotional senses previously experienced. Now ask the Spirit to tap your intuition and show you which of the following time periods produced the beneficial programs. Take notes if you desire.

- *Past lives:* Were you empathically skilled in regard to emotions in a previous life? Review application situations.

- *Epigenetics:* You might be borrowing your emotional skill from an ancestor. What or who pops into mind?

- *Family of origin:* Did your childhood family model emotional empathy? How did they model emotional sharing and caring? Note whatever they did that was positive.

- *Personal experiences:* Perhaps you've taught yourself about emotional empathy. What applicable knowledge have you acquired as you've moved through life?

Finally, summarize your observations, putting them into a single sentence that captures the reason you can perform emotional empathy so well.

For example, you might state: "I love registering others' emotions so they feel cared about."

STEP FOUR: **Recall a Negative.** It's time to unveil those pesky, not-so-useful emotional empathy programs. To accomplish this, remember a situation in which your emotional empathy resulted in overempathy, underempathy, or a manipulative situation. Request that the Spirit provide intuitive insights to reveal the causal situations that arose during the following time periods:

- *Past lives:* Did one or more past lives cause destructive emotional empathy wounds? Recall all pertinent situations.

- *Epigenetics:* Is an ancestor's experience torqueing your emotional boundaries? Ask the Spirit to help you intuitively perceive, see, hear, or know about any ancestral challenges.

- *Family of origin:* How did your childhood family distort your emotionally empathic boundaries? What did they model—or fail to model? How did you decide to conform to—or rebel against—their teachings?

- *Personal experiences:* Our life path might have created negative emotional programs. Concentrate on all pertinent situations until you have a strong sense of the events that might have warped your emotional boundaries.

Create a succinct statement that summarizes your emotional empathy weakness. For example, you might write: "I have to fix everyone's emotional problems to be safe."

STEP FIVE: **Design a New Program.** Reflect upon the positive and negative statements underlying the current state of affairs in regard to your emotional empathy. It's time to compose a newer and stronger belief, one that will accentuate your already-developed positive ideas and transform any negative ones. Ask that the Spirit help you generate this statement using the sentences you've already formulated. For instance, I would put the two ideas already presented in this exercise together this way:

"I'm happy to relate to another's emotions as long as I remain safe."

STEP SIX: **Cleanse and Renew Your Field.** It's cleaning time! Request that the Spirit use healing streams to wash away all negative programs and infuse your emotional empathy boundaries with the power of the new statement. Ask that these streams include any needed hues of orange, which will rejuvenate your physical and subtle bodies and fill in any energetic holes, injuries, or wounds.

STEP SEVEN: **Close.** When you feel restored, attend again to your everyday life.

TIP 7

❧

Free Those Feelings

It's easy to get snared in another's emotions. If you lack
the time needed to conduct the entirety of exercise 9,
"Deprogramming Your Emotional Empathy," conduct
Spirit-to-Spirit and request that the Spirit send orange
healing streams of grace to cleanse your system and
renew your emotional boundaries. Later, by using the
last exercise, you can dissect the reasons why you were
vulnerable.

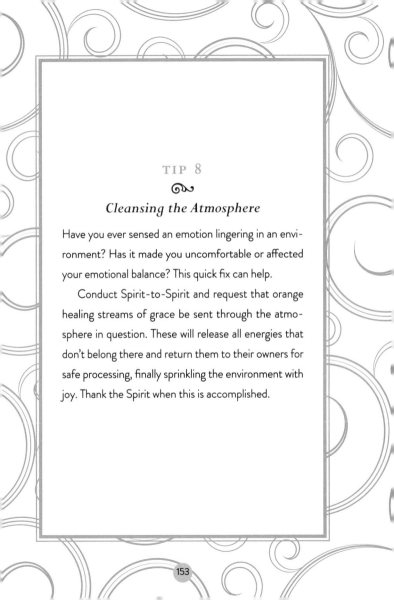

TIP 8

Cleansing the Atmosphere

Have you ever sensed an emotion lingering in an environment? Has it made you uncomfortable or affected your emotional balance? This quick fix can help.

Conduct Spirit-to-Spirit and request that orange healing streams of grace be sent through the atmosphere in question. These will release all energies that don't belong there and return them to their owners for safe processing, finally sprinkling the environment with joy. Thank the Spirit when this is accomplished.

Analyzing an Emotionally Empathic Message

How do you figure out the meaning of an emotionally empathic message? The following exercise will assist you with accomplishing this goal and also show you how to separate your feelings from another's feelings. If using it to analyze an emotionally charged group, simply turn the group into a singular entity in your head. Know that you can employ this exercise when relating to any living being, either during an empathic event or after one. I'll walk you through it as if you're assessing a current empathic event.

STEP ONE: **Become Aware.** Become aware of a received emotional message. Don't analyze it yet. You'll feel it as an emotion or a strong sensation stirring an internal emotional response.

STEP TWO: **Conduct Spirit-to-Spirit.** Affirm your spirit, the subject of the empathic message, all helping spirits, and the Spirit.

STEP THREE: **Assess the Message.** Request that the Spirit surround you, the message sender, and all concerned with healing streams. These streams will adjust the flow of information coming to you.

If it turns off the message, you weren't supposed to receive it. Ask for blessings for the sender, then continue with your day.

The incoming data might also lessen, increase, or remain the same. Simply trust the Spirit to make all necessary modifications, then ask that the Spirit separate your feelings from the subject's feelings. Promise that you'll address your own feelings later if they require personal attention. That task can be accomplished with tip 9, "Emotionally Caring for a Part of Yourself."

It's now time to assess the incoming information by asking the Spirit to provide you intuitive insights from the following areas:

- *Source of the data:* Who or what is sending the feelings you're noticing in your body? If you don't have an answer, simply skip this step.

- *What feelings are being shared?* There are five basic feeling constellations: anger, fear, sadness, disgust, and joy. See if what you're sensing fits within these categories or label them otherwise.

- ***What must be understood about the message?*** As covered on page 137, every feeling reflects a specific message. Ask the Spirit to let you intuitively sense what the subject needs, based on the feelings shared. Following is a prompt applicable to the five feeling constellations:

  ANGER: A boundary needs to be set. What is required?

  FEAR: There is a lack of safety. What action will create more safety?

  SADNESS: There is a need for more love. What will provide it?

  DISGUST: Someone or something is distasteful and unhealthy. What should be done?

  JOY: There is a positive situation occurring. How should it be recognized or celebrated?

- ***What should be done about the message?*** After focusing on the feelings and their meanings, ask the Spirit what you should do. There are a variety of choices, including the following:

- stating what you're sensing and running it by the subject

- sharing a word of assistance, advice, or support

- asking for healing streams to be sent directly to the subject

- simply feeling and energetically sending compassion

- asking questions of the subject

- asking the subject what they need from you

- physically mirroring the subject's emotions or physical behaviors

STEP FOUR: **Cleanse Yourself and Others.** When you feel finished with the interaction, ask that healing streams continue to work with you, the subject, and all concerned. In particular, run orange healing streams throughout the situation and your own boundaries.

STEP FIVE: **Close.** Return to your normal life when ready.

TIP 9

☙

Emotionally Caring for a Part of Yourself

If you want to further explore the feelings of a part of yourself, simply focus on that aspect and then request that the Spirit surround it in a bubble of orange healing streams. This enclosed self can now be treated like a person separate from you. When concluding the session, ask that the Spirit reintegrate that part of you into your overall self.

Whose Feelings Are They, Anyway?

One of the greatest challenges involved in emotional empathy is separating our personal feelings from those of others. When confused or overwhelmed, there are a few simple steps that can help. Use Spirit-to-Spirit before performing any of these undertakings:

Ask for Healing Streams

Request that the Spirit form a bubble around the subject's feelings with streams of grace and return the feelings to their spirit. Additional streams will then fill in your boundaries. You can trust that whatever emotions remain are your own to focus on and process.

Request a Percentage Split

Ask the Spirit to let you psychically hear or see a ratio showing what percentage of your internal emotions belong to you rather than someone (or something) else. Upon asking this question, psychically picture a circle with a vertical line drawn through its center. Ask the Spirit to imprint what percentage of the feelings belong to you on the left side, and on the right side the percentage that belongs to another. You can then request healing streams to release the other's emotions so you can focus on your own.

Hold a Stone

Grab a stone. I'd recommend a river rock, which energetically represents intuitive and emotional flow. You could also choose an orange-colored gemstone, such as carnelian or amber. Then request that the Spirit use healing streams to pour the feelings that belong to someone or something else into the stone. Ask that the Spirit use healing streams to wash the other's feelings through the stone and then restore them to their owner.

Shake or Wash Your Hands

Feelings are biochemically created within the physical body. Ask for healing streams to clean your body of others' feelings while you are shaking or washing your hands. Know that the streams will return their feelings to them in a life-enhancing way.

Ask for a Spiritual Guide

Sometimes we need to ask for help. Request that the spirit guides assisting you separate your emotions from those of others and help you understand why the merging occurred.

TIP 10

❧

When Flooded with Another's Feelings

What do you do if you're suddenly flooded with feelings that aren't your own? This event can be startling, especially if you have no idea whose emotions invaded your system. You can always conduct exercise 10, "Analyzing an Emotionally Empathic Message," but more quickly deal with the situation by following these steps:

STEP ONE: CONDUCT SPIRIT-TO-SPIRIT.
Affirm your spirit, other spirits, and the Spirit.

STEP TWO: ENCAPSULATE. Ask for healing streams to encapsulate the source's emotional energy and return it to their spirit.

STEP THREE: CLEANSE. Ask for orange healing streams for yourself. These will cleanse and then seal your empathic boundaries.

STEP FOUR: AWAIT. Ask that the Spirit relay any further actions to you.

• **EXERCISE 11** •

Relating to a Natural Being's Feelings

As already discussed in this chapter, natural beings—including animals and plants—have feelings. How might you sense the emotions of a pet, wild creature, tree, flower, or other type of natural being? How can you best analyze the sensation and respond accordingly? The following exercise will help you empathically tune into a living being and figure out a response.

STEP ONE: **Prepare.** Think about or relax near the living being you'd like to better understand.

STEP TWO: **Conduct Spirit-to-Spirit.** Affirm your spirit, the spirit of the subject, all helping spirits, and the Spirit.

STEP THREE: **Adjust with Healing Streams.** Ask for healing streams to adjust your empathic boundaries so you can relate to the natural being. Natural beings have vaster senses than we do, so we must stretch to relate to them.

STEP FOUR: **Ask to Receive.** Now request that the streams flow through the living being, lifting out their emotions so they can be safely shared with you.

STEP FIVE: **Receive Help with Relating.** Spend as much time as needed reflecting upon the being's emotions. Sense which ones might be categorized as anger, fear, sadness, disgust, or joy. Living beings have their own language, so you must request that the Spirit provide you supernatural insights into the emotions you're sensing. Let the Spirit attune you intuitively so you can understand the meaning of the empathic communiqués, and, if applicable, the needs of the living being. Needs can include care and tending, physical nourishment, companionship, understanding, or compassion.

STEP SIX: **Close with Compassion.** When it feels like you've comprehended and attended to the living being, ask the Spirit to send healing streams to the subject and to readjust your boundaries. Thank the Spirit for the help, then resume your everyday activities.

Analyzing by Body Area

Every area of the body vibrates at a unique frequency. Differing emotions also vibrate at distinct frequencies. This means that if you pay attention to the bodily area registering an empathically received emotion, you can figure out which feeling you've picked up from a subject.

The right and left sides of the body, as well as the lower, middle, and top third of the body, hold specific meanings. In the list I provide in this section, I'll share the meaning of these bodily regions as well as more specific bodily areas.

How will you know if you should pay attention to a certain part of the body? It will stand out from the rest. That bodily area (or region) might feel abnormally light, heavy, tingling, or filled with a celebratory or sharp sensation. You might also simply "know" what emotion is showing up. Trust your gut and use the list to further define an empathic message. You can then undergo exercise 10, "Analyzing an Emotionally Empathic Message," to further work with the empathic message.

Bodily Regions

Strong sensations or obvious emotions felt in the following bodily regions reflect the described issues:

RIGHT SIDE: Indicates feelings about actions, domination, or male issues.

LEFT SIDE: Reveals feelings related to intuition, receptivity, or female issues.

TOP THIRD: Sensations in the top of the chest upward are spiritual in nature.

MIDDLE THIRD: Stirrings between the upper abdomen and the top of the chest are psychologically based.

LOWER THIRD: Activity from the upper abdomen downward indicates earthy and material issues.

Bodily Areas

Obvious impressions or emotions felt in the following bodily areas can reflect feelings about these issues:

TOP OF THE HEAD: Spiritual connectivity.

BROW: Self-image or self-perception.

EARS: Messages about the self or the world.

EYES: How someone perceives the self, others, and the world.

THROAT: What has been or should be expressed.

BACK OF THE NECK: The principles guiding communication.

UPPER CHEST: Ability to express love.

MIDDLE CHEST: Ability to receive or give love.

SHOULDERS: Sense of being lovable.

ELBOWS: Space occupied in the world.

WRISTS: Maneuverability in the moment.

HANDS: What someone is holding onto or releasing.

RIBS: Protection.

SOLAR PLEXUS: Personal and positional power.

ABDOMEN: Deservedness to feel own feelings; creativity.

HIPS: Personal identity and the right to act.

GENITALS: Ability to exchange emotions through physical/sexual expression.

GROIN: Intimacy.

THIGHS: Parental memories.

KNEES: Movement forward; direction to take.

SHINS: Willingness to step onto the correct path of purpose.

CALVES: Willingness to be strong on the path of purpose.

ANKLES: Flexibility on the path of purpose.

FEET: Connection to the earth.

How might you work with the information provided about bodily regions and areas? Imagine that you're picking up on your cat's emotions in your right foot. The right side of the body is action-oriented. Feet relate to the connection to the earth. Your cat's feelings will have something to do with his ability to take action within his environment. Perhaps he's frustrated or sad because he can't go outside. You can assess his exact emotions and needs using exercise 10, "Analyzing an Emotionally Empathic Message."

Chapter Five

MENTAL EMPATHY
Taking an Instant Picture

Also called cognitive empathy, mental empathy allows us to clue into what others are thinking. You could say that mental empathy operates like a camera, taking instant flash pictures of another's perspective. It also plays a vital role in negotiating, making decisions, and pulling information from the universal mind, a cosmic reservoir of data.

This chapter will showcase how we can best encourage and smartly use this ability. After providing examples of mental empathy, I'll share its benefits and pitfalls. I'll next discuss the mechanics of this cognitive trait before furnishing techniques and tips aimed at putting this exciting mystical gift to good use.

Ideas and More Ideas
The Nature of Mental Empathy

Of the four types of empathy, mental empathy is the most difficult to grasp. How can you hold an idea in your hand or describe the precise color of a feeling? You can't. Nonetheless, your ability to relate to others' attitudes, thoughts, and perceptions depends on mental empathy.

Also called cognitive empathy, mental empathy can be experienced in several different ways. Maybe you can see yourself in some of the following stories:

- You're about to turn in a report when you freeze. You don't know how you know this, but you have to alter the premise to sell the proposal.

- There is something disturbing about the character of the person you just met. She seems friendly enough, but you sense she isn't honestly presenting her true thoughts.

- Your uncle sounds like he's complimenting your date, but you know better. You know that inside, your uncle is being racially judgmental.

- A negotiation is going south when you realize that you've been concentrating on *your* point of view. You tune into the potential partner and suddenly realize what you've been missing. The deal closes!

- It never fails: just when you really need to know something important, an idea pops into your brain. It's like you're plugged into a universal computer.

Mental empathy is the art of perspective-taking. It involves understanding another's mindset as if it's your own. Included is the ability to intellectually comprehend or mentally imagine another's perspective without fully engaging emotionally. When honed and developed, this skill can utilize abilities as far ranging as guessing, reasoning, and intuiting. And while we might sense another's emotions when we're operating mentally, we're able to keep another's feelings at bay and engage mind-to-mind.

Perhaps you can see why mental empathy is often called cognitive empathy. Cognition is the mental process involved in gathering and understanding knowledge. There are lots of tools required to be cognitive, which include knowing how to think. But we must also know how to acquire, break down, and analyze data, as well as store and remember memories. Then, with all this collected data, we can imagine and plan.

As you might deduce, there is all sorts of information that a mental empath can pick up on, including the following:

Another's Base of Knowledge

Through mental empathy we can access another's knowledge, which is provable or concrete data. Data is usually shared through speaking or writing, but during mental empathy it's psychically transferred from one person or being to another. For example, I once worked with an apprentice to a violin maker. This young man swore that he could absorb the craftsman's skills merely by sitting in his presence or thinking about the mentor.

Another's Perceptions and Paradigms

A perception is the impression or interpretation of something we're aware of. When we're attuning to another's perception, we're assessing their spin on a subject.

People arrive at perceptions through their paradigms. A paradigm is an accepted set of beliefs. A paradigm functions like eyeglasses that allow us to see situations a certain way. So basically, when we're empathizing with someone else's perceptions, we're checking out how they relate to a subject based on their beliefs.

When you're mentally empathizing, your perceptions might greatly differ from someone else's. Your job as an empath is to understand where someone else is coming from without losing your sense of self. For example, imagine that you like bowling. You take a friend bowling, and she doesn't like it. Are you going to feel hurt or are you going to try understanding her? Tuning into and asking questions of her—two activities you'll be taught to do in this chapter—let you discover that she's scared of the noise because she grew up in a chaotic family. You don't have to change your opinion to relate to your friend's perception, but you might have to bowl with a different friend.

Another's Mental Needs

It's not always enough to understand why someone perceives a situation a certain way. The next step involves meeting their cognitive needs. For example, I worked with a mom who was uncomfortable with her son's homosexuality. I sensed empathically that she lacked a scientific explanation for his innate sexual preference. I provided research for her to review. The data filled in the blanks for her, and she stopped being judgmental.

A Group's Mental Consciousness

In the last chapter I discussed emotional contagion, which occurs when feelings catch within a group of people. Thoughts can do the same, bonding people within a "group mind." A beneficial philosophy can glue people together for a good cause, such as to save the whales or eliminate world hunger. A destructive idea can cause great damage, such as the beliefs uniting members of a hate group.

Attunement to Natural Beings

Like humans, animals and other natural beings operate on mental patterns; we'll explore this fact in the next section. When we tune into a natural being's mental process, we can understand what they are going through and need.

For example, my sense is that my dog Lucky, the yellow Lab, avoids the vacuum cleaner because he thinks it's a monster that will eat him. After all, it gobbles up dirt! Honey, the golden retriever, on the other hand, likes the vacuum. He once saw it break down and gulp up a small cookie and is sure that someday the vacuum will cough up that treat.

Connection to the Universal Mind

Our individual brains are like computer terminals networked into a mainframe. We're able to link into, download information from, and upload data into the universal mind, a huge energetic net that contains all the knowledge that's ever been or ever will be known. We'll further explore this concept in the upcoming section "Mechanics of Mental Empathy."

What can we do with acquired mental knowledge? Above all, when we identify the thought processes of another living being, we can better relate to them. If we provide them feedback, they can better understand themselves, maybe even altering their approach and perceptions, should they choose. When we "get" someone, we can also more crisply negotiate with them.

Mental empathy is also key to developing social expertise and is especially useful during conversation. The gift also assists us in predicting another's behavior and protecting ourselves. As per the last comment, imagine that there is a difference between what someone says and what you sense they believe. Paying attention to your mental clues can keep you from being fooled.

You will know if you're using your mental empathy when you get a "gut sense," a sensation in the solar plexus that illuminates an understanding. Mental empathy can also be reflected as a sudden knowing of a fact that you've no reason to know or a voice that pops in your mind. The voice might sound like your own or someone else's, but it's always revealing something you didn't previously understand.

Sometimes we don't know we're being mentally empathic until we open our mouth and something smart and wise comes out. Other times, we simply sense what is happening with someone else or a group and either feel pulled toward or repulsed away from them.

As constructive as mental empathy sounds, it can also be distorted. Following are descriptions of its downsides:

Mental Overempathy

Overempaths often pay more attention to what others think or believe than their own thoughts. With porous empathic boundaries, they find themselves constantly attuning to others' perspectives and motivations but losing track of their personal opinions and needs. They might also be prone to fantasy, gathering so much information from others or the universal mind that they lose touch with reality.

For example, I once interacted with a teenage client who sparkled with bright and imaginative ideas. He claimed that these were fed him by all sorts of sources, including the "collective unconscious," Carl Jung's version of the universal mind, which I'll reference again in the next section. The problem was that he was flunking his classes because his brain was flying in the sky. Using the regiment of exercise 12, "Deprogramming Your Mental Empathy," I worked with his empathic boundaries and cleared up a hidden issue. He thought that by tapping into the illusory, he could avoid his social fears. Working through this tendency, he began passing his classes and fitting in at school.

Mental Underempathy

Underempaths fail to comprehend others' thoughts, beliefs, and mental needs, usually because they are caught up in their own opinions or are scared to get close to others. Some are trapped in a group mind, such as occurs with racism, sexism, and other forms of bigotry, while others are affected by specific genetic disorders, such as autism. If you're underempathic, stretch your boundaries and switch on your mental light. The exercises in this chapter will aid with this.

Mental Empathic Manipulation

Someone with a cold and calculating character can convince others that they care by figuring out and mirroring the subject's thinking patterns. Take a look at political leaders who represent discriminatory philosophies, such as racism or sexism. Frequently, they employ mental manipulation to create a group mind. To join, members often unwittingly disengage from their personal moral compass to follow the leader. On the other hand, the mentally deceived inadvertently fall prey to manipulators because they assume that the deceiver who is talking a good line is actually living that belief system.

You'll figure out the reasons you might be overempathic, underempathic, or involved in manipulation in exercise 12. Usually, however, our mental boundaries become distorted because of mentally challenging events or lack of proper modeling. For instance, overempaths often become that way if they are the family's problem-solver. Underempathy can happen when a family system is so chaotic that it seems safer to live in one's head. Underempathy can also be related to genetics.

Mechanics of Mental Empathy

The body of research that explains the specifics of mental empathy and how it operates distinctly from (and also with) emotional empathy is called Theory of Mind.

Theory of Mind explores the ways that we can understand the contents of another person's mind. It states that we can interpret someone's mental state, and even predict their behavior, based on our understanding of them. A mental state is made of a variety of factors, including thoughts, feelings, beliefs, desires, and the like. In essence, we can only truly comprehend another's mental state if we can "get inside their head," which is the task of mental empathy.

The basic theory is that we all have the potential to understand another's perceptions and predict what someone will be led to do, but only if we learned the following ideas when we were children:

- Another person's behavior is governed by their beliefs and desires. However, beliefs can be wrong and desires can go unfulfilled.

- People see reality from subjective rather than objective perspectives (Exploring Your Mind 2018).

Why do these ideas serve as cornerstones for developing healthy mental boundaries? If a child knows that another's reality is subjective, they won't blame themselves for someone else's negative perceptions and behaviors. They will know that the abusive or discriminatory adult or schoolyard bully is acting out their own issues and that their behaviors are not personal to them. They will also realize that bad treatment is always undeserved.

They'll comprehend that the beliefs and philosophies taught by schools, the family system, or places of worship aren't necessarily truth, and that ultimately, they can make their own logical and values-based decisions. In fact, I personally believe that most over- and underempathic distortions, as well as manipulative tendencies, could be at least partially corrected if everyone were raised to know that they have the right to form their own beliefs and paradigms and reject those that are unhealthy or create unhappiness.

Only when we know that someone else's thoughts and perceptions aren't about us, even if the other person insists that they are, can we paradoxically put aside our own mental constructs and comprehend another's mental state. Vital to this process is the ability to refrain from projecting on others or accepting others' projections.

As was first discussed in chapter 1, projection occurs when someone refuses to see their own issues and instead attributes them to others. Overempathizers tend to accept others' projections, as do the subjects of manipulators. Underempathizers and manipulators usually do the opposite, casting projections on others. I'll teach you a fast way to assess for projections in tip 11, "Checking for a Projection."

One way to free yourself from untrue mental empathy beliefs and projections is to open to the universal mind. The concept of a universal mind has been taught by cultures around the world and across time, but it also has been introduced into modern science. The basic theory is that we are all unified and sewn together through the consciousness of a higher force, or "God." Carl Jung, a deceased and well-known German psychologist, used the phrase "collective unconscious" to describe this unifying network, which is populated by symbols and archetypes that influence our personal psyche. In more recent years, Lynne McTaggart, a scientist and author, calls this intertwining reality "the Field," considering it a force made of light that interconnects us all (McTaggart 2008). When we are attuned to this force, our systems balance and we interconnect with others in healthy ways. When we're not in tune, illness and mental imbalance ensue.

We interact with—and create with the light emanating from—this field through intention. Intention is the ability to direct our thoughts. Mental empathy allows us to relate to others' thoughts; however, we don't want to be steered by them, as most thoughts are negative or dysfunctional and we certainly don't want to create our ideas—or reality—based on negative thoughts. Because of this, it's important to create a relationship with this field or the universal mind and evaluate our own and others' opinions based on what matches with its highest light. You'll be shown how to do this in exercise 13 and tip 13.

Just as you can mentally interact with other people, so can you happily do the same with other natural beings. As pointed out by author Carl Safina throughout his book *Beyond Words*, animals definitely exhibit consciousness and developed mental states. The fact that they show behavioral and food preferences, interact, play, make choices, and learn is proof positive that they are conscious (Safina 2016). Even honeybees are respected for their mental intelligence; they actually understand the concept of zero, which is only true of a few species (Georgiou 2018).

And now it's time to experience *your* mental empathy.

• EXERCISE 12 •

Deprogramming Your Mental Empathy

Programs are the beliefs that run your system. To employ your mental empathy gift wisely and safely, your empathic boundaries must be managed by healthy programs. In this exercise you'll assess your current programs, both positive and negative, and also use the color yellow to establish life-enhancing boundaries. Yellow represents personal power and structure. You need both attributes to make good use of your mental empathy. You'll use this color in the following exercise.

STEP ONE: **Prepare.** Select a quiet space for this exercise. Grab writing equipment to keep track of your findings.

STEP TWO: **Conduct Spirit-to-Spirit.** Affirm your spirit, all the helping spirits—including any linked to the people that have affected your mental boundaries—and the Spirit.

STEP THREE: **Remember a Positive.** Most likely, you've experienced several high points with your mental empathy. Ask the Spirit to grant you psychic pictures, senses, and messages from the positive circumstances that affected you during the following time periods:

- *Past lives:* Is there a past life in which you applied your mental empathy toward a beneficial end? Check to see which memories arise.

- *Epigenetics:* Through the mists of time there might be an ancestor who employed their mental empathy in powerful ways. See who comes into mind and assess what made their empathic powers so advantageous for you. There might be multiple ancestors. Simply interact energetically with those who appear.

- *Family of origin:* How did your family model mental boundaries? In what ways did your relatives mentor your mental insights? Get a sense of the constructive events.

- *Personal experiences:* Life teaches us what we need to know. What have you figured out in terms of your mental empathy that has been useful to-date?

- Summarize your findings in one sentence that encompasses your positive mental empathy programs. For example, you might write: "I attune to another's motivations when it is useful for all parties involved."

STEP FOUR: **Recall a Negative.** It's time to explore the negative programs that are forging your mental boundaries. Request that the Spirit gift you intuitively formed images, messages, or bodily awarenesses in relation to the programming experiences that occurred in the following time periods:

- *Past lives:* We carry past life influences into each subsequent lifetime. See if recollections from previous lives enter your mind upon reflecting on negative mental empathy events.

- *Epigenetics:* Ancestors' experiences can transfer into our own body, causing dehumanizing mental empathy patterns. What relevant insights pop into your head?

- *Family of origin:* Perhaps your childhood family negatively influenced your mental boundaries. If so, what happened that caused distorted boundaries? What occurred—or didn't—that set the groundwork for destructive mental empathy patterns?

- *Personal experiences:* Your own life experiences might have harmed your mental boundaries. Muse over whatever you have gone through.

Create a one-sentence summary of your negative mental experiences. For example: "I believe it's my job to fix everyone's mental state."

STEP FIVE: **Forge a New Program.** Examine the negative and positive statements you've forged and merge them into a single and beneficial statement that will keep the positive energies flowing and disintegrate the negative. Using the sentences already presented in this exercise, I might write the following: "When everyone benefits, including myself, I can attune to another's mental state."

STEP SIX: **Cleanse and Make Anew Your Field.** Let's sweep away all those pesky negatives! Request that the Spirit use a divine broom made of healing streams to cleanse your soul and body across time. While sending others' energies back to them with love, these beams will employ various hues of yellow to clear and rejuvenate your empathic boundaries. All aspects of you will be programmed with the uplifting mental programs you've just developed.

STEP SEVEN: **Close.** When finished, send gratitude to the Spirit and return to your normal life.

❧

Checking for a Projection

Are you being projected on? Are you projecting on someone else? How can you tell? Conduct exercise 12, "Deprogramming Your Mental Empathy," and when evaluating for negative programs during step four, ask the Spirit if you perform projections. If you do, address that fact when writing up the summative sentence. For instance, in the example provided, you can write, "I believe it's my job to fix everyone's mental state by accepting another's projections." Or you could say, "I project onto others as a way of figuring out their mental state." Then address that part of the programming when writing a fix-it statement in step five.

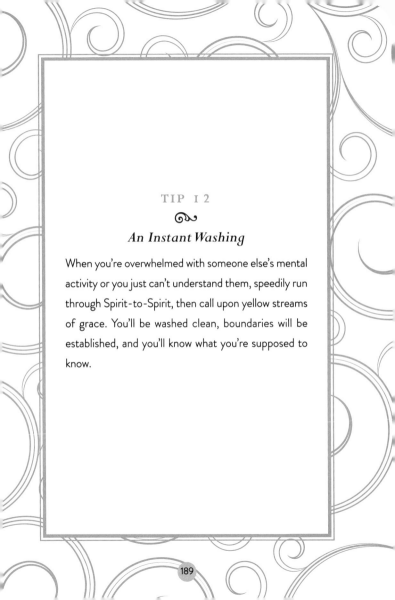

TIP 12

⟳

An Instant Washing

When you're overwhelmed with someone else's mental activity or you just can't understand them, speedily run through Spirit-to-Spirit, then call upon yellow streams of grace. You'll be washed clean, boundaries will be established, and you'll know what you're supposed to know.

Analyzing a Mentally Empathic Message

How do you best analyze a mental message? The following exercise, which you'll perform in real time, will assist you in accomplishing this goal. You can also apply it to a prior mental empathy experience. If addressing a previous empathic episode, simply run through the following steps as if the experience is currently happening.

STEP ONE: **Become Aware.** Assess how you're receiving a mental communication. Mental messages register as a knowing, awareness, mental idea, or internal voice. The voice might sound like your own or another's.

STEP TWO: **Conduct Spirit-to-Spirit.** Affirm your spirit, the spirit sending the communiqué, all the helping spirits, and the Spirit.

STEP THREE: **Assess the Message.** Ask that the Spirit encompass you, the message's sender, and all involved in the communication with healing streams. These will fine-tune the flow of data you're receiving. If the spigot turns off, you aren't supposed to be involved in this mental exchange.

Request blessings for the sender, ask that the streams completely release you from this interchange, and continue with your world.

If the incoming information lessens or increases, the Spirit has made adjustments for you. If it remains the same, so be it. You can now ask that the Spirit distinguish between your mental state and the sender's mental state. You'll sense yourself separating from the incoming mental data but still be able to register what you're taking in. Next, request that the Spirit provide you intuitive insights, which might be psychically visual, verbal, or sensory, to assess the following arenas of information:

Source of the data: Who or what is the source of the mental information? If there isn't an answer, skip this step and move onward.

What knowledge is being shared: There are many types of information provided about an empathic sender through mental empathy. A few are listed here:

- ideas (usually the sender's ideas about a topic)

- perceptions (often the sender's perspective about a subject or situation)
- the reasons for a perspective, such as a historical event or a cultural viewpoint
- mental needs
- motivations
- an overarching mental state or condition
- mental disturbances
- beliefs and opinions
- judgments and prejudices
- causes of fears, shame, and other emotions
- reasons for low self-esteem or low self-confidence
- insights, knowledge, or wisdom that you (the recipient) needs, either for yourself or to better understand the subject
- the sender's reactions to a mental idea

What must be understood about the message:
This step requires that you connect with the Spirit or the sender's spirit to know what to do with the mental data. Simply take a few deep breaths and ask the Spirit how you are to interpret the data received. The response might involve a gut sense, a psychic image or word, or some other form of knowing.

Ask the universal mind: You can also ask the Spirit to assist you in tapping into the universal mind, which will issue you an insight.

What should be done about the message: Query the Spirit about how you are to best respond to the interpreted mental information. There are a lot of choices, which can include any of the following:

- speak aloud about the underlying meaning of the received message
- verbally acknowledge the sender's point of view
- send compassion while remaining silent

- ask questions; curiosity is key to helpful mental empathy (see exercise 14, "Creating the Curious Questioner," to come up with helpful questions)

- ask the sender what they need from you

- share your own beliefs and then compare them aloud with your interpretation of the sender's perceptions

- highlight the similarities between your thoughts and the subject's thoughts

- state the differences between your point of view and the subject's point of view

- mirror the subject's emotions or physical behaviors

STEP FOUR: **Cleanse Yourself and Others.** When the interchange is finished, request healing streams for all concerned.

STEP FIVE: **Close.** Continue with your normal life when ready.

TIP 13

⟡

Tapping Into the Universal Mind

Want to easily tap into the universal mind for a purpose or just for fun? Perform Spirit-to-Spirit and ask the Spirit to directly plug a stream of grace from the universal mind into your brain. Ask that the Spirit assist you in interpreting the information flowing in, and thank the Spirit for the resulting insights. Cleanse your boundaries with yellow healing streams of grace when finished.

Mentally Relating to a Part of Yourself

Sometimes we have to get in touch with an aspect of ourselves that needs to be understood. Examples include an inner child, a past-life self, a part of the self apparent during a dream, or an adult self that went through a celebratory or challenging experience. Simply surround this self in a bubble made of healing streams and relate to it as subject of exercise 13, "Analyzing a Mentally Empathic Message." Focus on mental knowledge and perception. When finished, ask for this self to be lovingly reintegrated into your greater self during step four, when you are cleansing yourself and others.

Stripping Beliefs to Their Core

All mental states, conditions, and beliefs reduce to one of two major paradigms. The first reflects a state of being connected. The second can be summarized as being disconnected, or believing oneself to be separate.

When someone feels connected—to the universe, the Spirit, others, or themselves—their mental state and perceptions will reflect the truth of love. Their mental condition will be primarily positive and optimistic. When someone believes themselves disconnected, however, their perceptions are more negative and pessimistic.

To analyze where someone is coming from, let the Spirit help you sense which core belief explains the subject of your mental empathy. If the subject has a connected mental state, you might receive sensations that make you feel uplifted, upbeat, and trusting. Images will be light and sunny in nature, and verbal indications will be confident and buoyant. If a subject is stricken with a negative mental state, your gut reactions to them will leave you feeling heavy, depressed, and mistrusting. Psychic visions will be dark and shadowy, and verbal intuitions will be downbeat and discouraging.

Your conclusion will help you evaluate the health of the subject's mental state and know how to act accordingly. For instance, if a person is more connected than not, they are probably thinking rationally and with heart. You can be more open and communicative with them. If they think of themselves as separate—from themselves, goodness, other people, or the Spirit—tread lightly. If led, find a way to assist them in examining their viewpoints, and above all, be compassionate.

• EXERCISE 14 •

Creating the Curious Questioner

When you're attuning to the mental state of a subject, you want to understand them as deeply as possible. Comprehension creates the basis for cross-learning, negotiating for a common end, and deciding how to provide aid, care, and education. To achieve these outcomes, this exercise will employ three skills.

The first is called "radical listening." It includes understanding what someone is verbally stating and what you are mentally sensing, but also making sure that the subject knows that you get them.

The second vital aptitude is to hold two opinions (your own and the subject's) at the same time. This is especially important if you carry a different belief than the subject does. The trick is to validate yourself and the subject while concentrating on the topic.

The third ability is to develop curiosity. Curiosity is the secret to developing the other two described skills.

So let's turn on your quizzical self in such a way that you also learn how to radically listen and multitask perceptions.

You'll initially practice this goal with a partner to help you develop the imbedded mental empathy techniques. You can then use these skills at any other time.

To begin, select a trusted friend who has a mental issue or perception that they would like to better understand and that they are willing to let you delve into. Now get sleuthing!

STEP ONE: **Prepare.** Seclude yourself and your partner in a quiet place. Sit in chairs facing each other. Then ask your partner to reflect upon a situation that has cost them mental peace.

STEP TWO: **Conduct Spirit-to-Spirit.** Affirm your spirit, your partner's spirit, all helping spirits, and the Spirit.

STEP THREE: **Listen.** Ask your partner to talk about their focus and explain it to you. Mirror them physically, leaning forward when they do, bobbing your head when they do, and so on. Mutter affirmatively as you're listening. Perform the next step simultaneously.

STEP FOUR: **Sense.** At the same time that you're listening to and mirroring your partner, give permission for the Spirit to help you intuitively sense the flow of mental data coming from your partner. Request that the Spirit adjust the intensity and contents with healing streams, which you can picture as yellow, so that you can register rather than hold on to the information. Energetically mirror or become one with the information to whatever level is safe for you.

STEP FIVE: **Encapsulate.** Radical listening—and sensing—begins and ends by sharing with the other person what you are hearing and sensing. Summarize what they are saying and keep asking if you're getting it right. Also run your intuitive musings by them. Alter your feedback until your partner is stating that they feel understood.

STEP SIX: **Question.** What questions spring into mind about what your subject has shared? It's time to be curious. The purpose of these questions is to deepen your understanding of the reasons why they believe what they believe. You can even ask the Spirit to provide you questions. The Spirit's questions will either pop in your mind or come out of your mouth, formed by the Spirit, when you speak. Potential questions include the following:

- What occurred in your history to create your beliefs?
- How important is this topic to you and why?
- How does this topic affect you?
- How would you summarize your perceptions in a single sentence?
- How do you deal with people who think differently than you do?

STEP SEVEN: **Evaluate Within.** Pause and spend a moment reflecting on your subject's topic. Concentrate on your own related beliefs and perceptions. Fully embrace them. Now accept your own and your partner's point of view simultaneously. Hold both areas of knowledge as equally important while deciding you'll continue focusing on your partner.

STEP EIGHT: **Complete the Conversation.** Continue visiting with your partner, and see if there is anything to clear up or further address.

STEP NINE: **Close.** When finished, thank your partner, letting healing streams separate your boundaries, and tuck away all that you've learned from this interaction.

When to Shut Down

It's important to know that we're in charge of our mental empathy faculties and that we don't have to use our empathic skills if we don't want to. Conduct Spirit-to-Spirit and ask the Spirit to block another's energy while supporting your empathic boundaries if any of the following occurs:

- You feel endangered or threatened emotionally, mentally, or physically.

- The other person scares you.

- You sense you're being tricked.

- You don't have the energy to help.

- There is too much dissonance between what the subject is saying and you are sensing.

- You know you won't be respected for your own viewpoint.

- You don't think you can respect the other's viewpoint.

- The other's mental state is questionable; perhaps they are mentally ill or confused.

- You think you are being projected upon.

- The other person is stuck in a fantasy.

Mental Tricks for
Voicing an Empathic Sense

There are three "voicing" tricks for sharing mentally empathic data.

Thought to Voice

You can turn a mental stream into words by conducting Spirit-to-Spirit and then concentrating on your solar plexus, one of the main chakra areas that process mentality. Picture the color yellow and ask that healing streams shift the body-based knowledge upward and into your throat. Then begin to speak, letting words flow out of your mouth. You'll automatically voice what you're perceiving.

Thought to Paper

Gather writing instruments. After performing Spirit-to-Spirit, bring your attention to your solar plexus. Ask that yellow streams of grace lift the empathic knowledge into your heart. Let the words emerge onto the paper through your hands. Whatever you read will contain the nugget of sought wisdom.

Spirit to Throat

Carry out Spirit-to-Spirit when relating mentally and request that the Spirit send the appropriate words to share through your mouth from the back side of your neck. Open—and let the Spirit speak. Remain aware of your subject's reactions so you are tuned into the conversation that follows.

Now it's time to examine the last type of spiritual empathy, the one devoted to light.

Chapter Six

SPIRITUAL EMPATHY
Lighting Up with Light

Nothing is more powerful than light. Light enables the viewing of what lies within us and others, and it is the tool of the spiritual empath, who can perceive the light in others.

Spiritual empathy is the ultimate honor. Through it we can resonate with another's core nature, purpose, gifts, insights, and destiny. The "other" can include a living person but also the deceased, invisible beings and guides, and the Spirit. While our focus is on perceiving a subject's light, we can also spot shadows and the dark.

As we proceed with this chapter, I'll give examples of spiritual empathy and discuss the types of beings and energies it invites connection to. We'll look at the ways that we can be positively but also negatively affected by spiritual empathy, and then jump into the techniques and tips section of the chapter.

As compared to previous chapters, this one will not cover mechanics. That's because there isn't a measurable way to describe spiritual empathy. Essentially, the gift is performed by connecting our spirit to other spirits, and this process isn't easy to quantify. Know that mirror neurons and energetic fields are just as involved in the process as they are in other forms of empathy, but something more magical twinkles in the spiritual empathy process. You see, when a practice is about light, the light does the work.

What Can You See with the Light?

Imagine you've been handed an enchanted flashlight. No one knows you're holding it, but when you shine it upon someone, wonder ensues. You become aware of their inner light, or essence. You glimpse their life purpose, spiritual gifts, and destiny. You deliver inspiration and insights. You can also assess how closely they are actively expressing their professed value system and living in alignment with truth.

And that's just the initial description of the kaleidoscope of spiritual empathy.

Change the lens and you can perceive the essence of a natural being, as well as supernatural entities. You can also obtain and share revelatory insights, spiritual wisdom, and messages from the deceased. As well, you can operate prophetically, which involves knowing what the Spirit knows, as if you are occupying the same "mind space."

Just as light reveals what is pure, so does it showcase the dark and shadowy. Because of this, spiritual empathy can discern the differences between beneficial and harmful beings and even release someone from an overcasting evil.

If you put yourself in the following stories, you'll see what I mean.

- You have a special gift, but you don't know what to call it. Within a few minutes, you can usually get a sense of someone's unique gifts and what they might do with them.

- Why isn't it apparent to others? You can tell the man is lying, even though he sounds logical.

- There is a room in your house that you won't go into. It's tainted. Something evil hovers in there.

- You and your dog have the same power: you both know who to trust or not. The hairs stand up on your arm, as do the hackles on your dog.

- Are they angels? You don't know, but some sort of supernatural figures relay messages to you for others.

Spiritual empathy is the pinnacle of empathy because ultimately, we're all spirits seeking to become conscious of what really counts, which is love. Consequently, the highest forms of spiritual empathy allow subjects to feel more loved, loveable, and loving. As already explained, this applies to people but also a plethora of other beings. Examine the following short list and you'll see who or what you can connect to and how you might empathically perceive a spiritual message.

Another (Living) Person's Spiritual Essence

Everyone has—and is—a spirit, a vital spark knowingly connected to the Spirit. Spiritual empathy allows you to link with another person's spirit. You might perceive their ultimate purpose, value system, spiritual gifts, and heart-based needs, and also determine if they are living in concert with this genuine self.

For example, imagine that you're talking with two accountants about their jobs. When one woman shares, your own spirit soars. You psychically envision sunshine. These spiritually empathic insights tell you that Subject One is aligned with her spirit and using her innate abilities. When the other woman converses, though, you feel glum and low-spirited. The vision of a storm cloud invades your mind. These body-based sensations convey that Subject Two is out of alignment.

Perhaps your prophetic gift goes one step further: what floats in but an image of Subject Two in a lab coat. You ask Spirit if there is a good way to share that she could consider a job in the medical profession.

I'll share more about the types of gifts you can spot in others in this chapter's exercise 17, "Uncovering Another's Spiritual Gifts."

A (Living) Natural Being's Spiritual Essence

All living beings have a spirit. Using spiritual empathy, you can sense a living being's core nature, needs, and purpose. For instance, your prophetic gift might suggest that your cat soothes emotions or that your goldfish represents beauty. Maybe you even perceive the story of a gemstone that assists in healing work. As with tuning into people, empathizing with a natural being is accomplished through conscious awareness. You simply become aware or picture what is to be understood spiritually.

Deceased and Otherworldly Beings, Human and Natural

People and beings who have died or dwell on nonworldly planes of existence are available to the spiritual empath. There are two basic divisions of these beings.

BEINGS OF LIGHT: These are motivated to create love. They might reveal themselves to the empath in order to deliver inspiration, revelation, or life-enhancing messages to a subject. For instance, a deceased relative might reach through the veil to give advice, a spiritual master might relay wisdom, or an angel could dispense a warning. How do you know that a being is connecting with your empathic senses? Beings of light will feel elevating, godly, and kind. They might present themselves through psychic visons or verbal messages when you're awake or asleep. They can also be noticed as positive energies in a room.

BEINGS OF DARK: Dark beings are those that prey upon the living. I also call them "interference" since ultimately, they interfere with a victim's spiritual purpose and expression. You'll psychically perceive them as shadowy, black, or brackish in coloration, and if they speak, their voice will grate on you, leaving you feeling frenetic or off-kilter. Plain and simple, dark beings are creepy and scary. When operating prophetically, you might pick up on the interference attached to an aspect of yourself or more likely to your empathic subject.

Connection to the Spirit

The prophet can sense a subject's connection to the Spirit and is led to help them establish a cleaner bond. For instance, I once worked with an older woman who didn't feel worthy of a romantic relationship. We tracked the issue back to her mother's overzealous religiosity, which was the basis of unmercifully shaming messages. Once we cleared the mother's negative effects, which took several sessions, my client was able to sense the presence of the greater Spirit. After about a year of enjoying the flow of energy between herself and the Spirit, she felt worthy of a relationship. She met a lovely person and has now been in that relationship for several years.

Unfortunately, there are a lot of negative issues that can affect the spiritual empath, mainly due to distorted boundaries. Here are a few of the hazards:

Spiritual Overempathy

Overempaths can be so aware of another's spiritual needs, values, or issues that they ignore their own. For instance, I worked with a woman who reported to a racist boss. She sensed that he was against biracial relationships, so she didn't display pictures of her biracial son. She was so overconcerned about her boss's attitude, which she perceived through her spiritual empathy, that she disregarded her son. As we adjusted her empathic boundaries, which you'll do using exercise 15, "Deprogramming Your Spiritual Empathy," she began to reveal her life. She put a picture of herself and her son on her desk and ignored her boss's issues.

Overempaths can also be very sensitive to others who aren't expressing their stated values. This awareness can lead to judgmentalism. For instance, I had a female client who constantly picked on her husband because he drank a couple of beers on the weekends, even though he detested alcoholics. She was overcritical of the differences between his belief and his actions, and her nagging caused problems in their relationship. Because he didn't actually have an alcohol problem, she backed off and they got along better. As this story infers, spiritual empaths sometimes need to keep their "spiritual business" out of another's business.

Another downside to spiritual overempathy can be a vulnerability to otherworldly beings. I could share a thousand stories to prove this point, such as a child who couldn't sleep more than a few hours because she saw ghosts in her room; an electrician who had so many deceased electricians boss him around that he was going mad; the CEO who could hear the deceased connected to his employees; and the husband who saw demons attached to shoppers at the grocery store. They all deserved more privacy, which they acquired through practices similar to that featured in exercise 15.

Spiritual Underempathy

Spiritual underempaths find it difficult or impossible to attune to another's spirit, connect with the "other side," or accurately perceive another's value system. This can lead to spiritual isolation or incomplete relationships. And an underempath in the position of authority can also cause problems for others. For instance, consider the underempathic boss who refuses to give his employees time off to observe a religious holiday. The employees will feel unsupported and judged.

Spiritually Empathic Manipulation

It's extremely dangerous to be spiritually manipulative or manipulated. From my point of view, Hitler's overtaking of the German people fundamentally involved spiritual manipulation. The aftermath of World War I saw a people defeated financially but also spiritually. Hitler offered them a spiritual paradigm—called Nazism—to fill the hole. It's well-documented that Hitler had a demonic advisor who fed him horrid ideas.

Being spiritually manipulated leads to deep inadequacy and self-doubt, as well as a lack of self-worthiness.

Cult victims are an example. While the cult leader offers a spiritual belief system promising a sense of meaning, the principles are nothing more than a ship's plank positioned over shark-infested waters.

It can be terribly difficult to defeat spiritual manipulation, no matter which side of the fence it's occurring on. That's because dark beings are attracted to spiritual deceivers and victims. The ultimate goal of a dark entity is to steal the light from either group of people, thus avoiding its own relationship with the Spirit. Perhaps it is scared of God's judgment; maybe the entity enjoys harming others. Either way, you'll learn how to search for and release dark spirits in exercise 18, "Lighting Up the Dark."

What can torque our spiritual boundaries? Sometimes the tendency is a carryover from a past life. For instance, many overempaths were often healers, intuitives, counselors, priests, or people who used their spiritual abilities to assist others. What might have worked thousands of years ago isn't as helpful now. When an overempath continues a past-life pattern of "helping," they can too easily become overwhelmed with others' needs. After all, the world is busier and more populated.

Underempathy can also be caused by past-life influences. The current-day underempath might have been incredibly empathic during an earlier life, except they were punished for their gift. If hung, tortured, killed, or shamed for their prophetic ability, a soul might abstain from spiritual connectivity now.

Family-of-origin issues affect all empaths, including the spiritually empathic. I was an overempath as a child because my ability to see, sense, and hear spirits kept me safe. They would soothe me at night and alert me to my mother's moods. My father was an underempath despite the fact that his mother could talk to ghosts, because he was scared of what he couldn't control.

No matter what, we all deserve to enjoy our spiritual connectivity, which you'll learn how to accomplish through the following techniques and tips.

• EXERCISE 15 •

Deprogramming Your Spiritual Empathy

Destructive spiritual programs can prevent you from tuning into your own or another's true nature and separate you from the spiritual universe. Through this exercise you'll analyze your positive and negative spiritual programs and employ the color white, which represents purity and spiritual power, to create love-based empathic boundaries.

STEP ONE: **Prepare.** Bring writing instruments into a quiet space and relax.

STEP TWO: **Conduct Spirit-to-Spirit.** Affirm your spirit, all the helping spirits, spirits connected to anyone that has affected your spiritual boundaries, and the Spirit.

STEP THREE: **Remember a Positive.** At some point, you employed your spiritual empathy wisely and fruitfully. Let the Spirit grant you intuitive images, senses, and messages indicating the reasons for the healthy spiritual responses developed during the following time periods:

- *Past lives:* In which past lives did you excel at spiritual empathy? See what arises for you.

- *Epigenetics:* Most likely, at least one of your ancestors was a spiritual empath or prophet. Get a sense of who they were, what they did, and how their experiences have constructively impacted you.

- *Family of origin:* In what ways did your family of origin instruct you in proper spiritual boundaries and leave you with a strong sense of your own spirit? How did they help develop your consciousness and conscience? Write down what you remember.

- *Personal experiences:* Record what life experiences established the latticework for your prophetic powers.

Summarize your findings in a single sentence showcasing the positive programs. For example, you might write: "I sense others' spiritual gifts so they can best achieve them."

STEP FOUR: **Recall a Negative.** What events created negative spiritual programs? Let the Spirit tap your psychic senses to relay images, senses, and messages to answer the question from the perspective of the following time zones:

- *Past lives:* Record any past-life experiences that established harmful spiritual programs.

- *Epigenetics:* Adverse ancestral experiences can cost us healthy spiritual boundaries. What does your intuition show you?

- *Family of origin:* Our family system is frequently the main source of negative spiritual programs. Relay as many memories as you can when writing.

- *Personal experiences:* Our responses to life events can bring about damaging spiritual beliefs. What pops into your mind in this regard?

Formulate a sentence that summarizes your negative spiritual programs. Maybe you write: "I have to ignore invisible spirits or my family will think I'm weird."

STEP FIVE: **Create a New Program.** Review the two statements you've written and arrive at a wonderful new belief that will allow only healthy spiritual boundaries. Employ the sentences from this exercise. For instance, I could use the sentences already created to form the following statement:

"I can employ my own senses or input from safe spirits to tune into other's spiritual gifts."

STEP SIX: **Wash and Reset Your Field.** It's now time for the Spirit to erase any negative programs and repair your empathic boundaries. Request that the Spirit employ healing streams toward this end and cleanse you with white, the color of purity. Focus simultaneously on the new belief. All aspects of you will be continually renewed and connected to the Spirit forevermore.

STEP SEVEN: **Close.** When complete, return to your normal life.

ॐ

An Instant Spiritual Cleansing

Are you spiritually overwhelmed, spiritually blocked, or involved in a manipulative situation? Recite Spirit-to-Spirit and ask for white healing streams. These will clean and renew all your boundaries and connect you directly to the Spirit.

• **EXERCISE 16** •

Analyzing a Spiritually Empathic Message

How can you assess a spiritual message? Whether it emanates from a living person, a natural being, or an otherworldly spirit, the steps are the same. You can walk through this exercise with a message in mind, but you can also use it for a previously experienced spiritual experience.

STEP ONE: **Become Conscious.** Focus on a spiritual communication, which might be recognized as a conscious awareness, a prophetic revelation, an image, or a psychically verbal message.

STEP TWO: **Conduct Spirit-to-Spirit.** Affirm your spirit, the subject or messenger's spirit, surrounding spirits, and the Spirit.

STEP THREE: **Analyze the Message.** Let the Spirit surround you with healing streams, which will be primarily white. These will either shut down the flow of data, keep it the same, or otherwise adjust it for the safety of all. If the stream disappears, bless all involved, clean your energy with white, and return to your day. Otherwise, request that the Spirit encapsulate the incoming information and set it within a ball of white light, which will operate like a crystal ball.

Picture the ball in your mind's eye, seeing it at about your heart level. Gaze into it with your psychic eyes and examine the visions inside to uncover the following information:

- *Source of the data:* If you don't already know, ask from who or what the information is streaming. If the answer isn't clear, simply continue. (If you are connecting with an otherworldly being, use the ideas shared in tip 17 during this step.)

- *What knowledge is being shared:* A being's spirit can reveal just about anything, including information about purpose, spiritual needs, spiritual gifts, destiny, upcoming choices, a correct decision, guidance, revelation, insight, inspiration, and warnings. You can use exercise 17, "Uncovering Another's Spiritual Gifts," to more completely comprehend messages about spiritual gifts.

- *What must be understood about the message:* Let the Spirit deepen your understanding about the message and why it's important. If you internally mirror, request that the Spirit employ hues of white to keep you and your subject safe.

- *What should be done about the message:* Request that the Spirit show you how to respond to the spiritually received message. Continue psychically peering into the crystal ball, but also read your own heart. Choices can include the following:

  - state aloud your sense of the received message
  - check out your conclusions with the sender, if possible
  - remain quiet and simply care
  - hold a conversation with the subject or the subject's spiritual guide, if applicable
  - ask questions

- ask the sender what they need from you
- physically mirror the subject's emotions or behaviors, if applicable

STEP FOUR: **Cleanse the Crystal Ball.** When the conversation is finished, request bright white healing streams for all concerned, and allow these to dissipate the crystal ball.

STEP FIVE: **Close.** All will be well as you continue your everyday life.

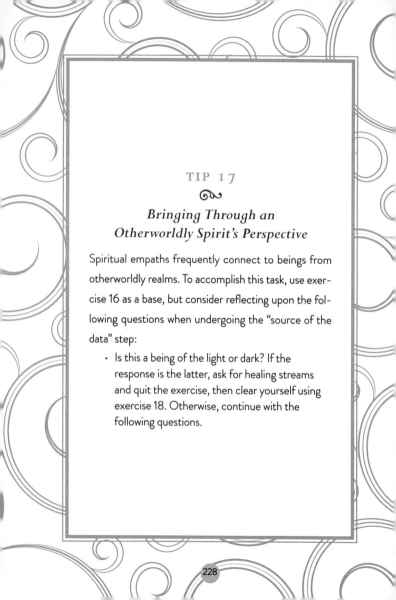

TIP 17

Bringing Through an
Otherworldly Spirit's Perspective

Spiritual empaths frequently connect to beings from
otherworldly realms. To accomplish this task, use exercise 16 as a base, but consider reflecting upon the following questions when undergoing the "source of the
data" step:

- Is this a being of the light or dark? If the
  response is the latter, ask for healing streams
  and quit the exercise, then clear yourself using
  exercise 18. Otherwise, continue with the
  following questions.

- Is this a deceased being? If so, was it once a person or some other type of natural being?
- Is this a soul you've known before, such as in a past life?
- Is this the soul of a relative or a once-known person?
- Is this the soul of a natural being you've known before?
- Is this soul one that will be entering the earth plane, maybe becoming a child in the future?
- Is this a purely spiritual being, such as an angel or a master, which is a being that serves a higher function?
- Is this a soul from another plane or planet?
- Is this an aspect of the Spirit itself?

Continue to reflect upon the source of this message.

TIP 18

∿

Spiritually Relating to a Part of Yourself

I love using exercise 16, "Analyzing a Spiritually Empathic Message," when working with a past-life self, an inner child, or directly relating to my spirit, such as I do when making a destiny-based decision. All you have to do is put yourself in the crystal ball in that particular exercise and perform all other steps. When concluding the exercise, ask the Spirit to integrate the "you" inside the crystal ball back into your current identity, even as the crystal ball disintegrates.

• **EXERCISE 17** •

Uncovering Another's Spiritual Gifts

One of the most exciting applications of spiritual empathy is uncovering another's spiritual gifts, the special abilities enabling a spirit to fulfill its mission during this lifetime. This short exercise will help you define another's specific spiritual gifts.

STEP ONE: **Conduct Spirit-to-Spirit.** Acknowledge your spirit, all involved spirits, and the Spirit.

STEP TWO: **Request Illumination.** Ask that the Spirit link you with the person you'd like to assess and indicate their major gift or gifts. You might see a light shine psychically upon a specific choice, receive a bodily awareness, or hear an intuitive response. The main choices are as follows:

- *Physical gifts:* Exhibited by those who are physically skilled, highly active, or good with finances, money, the environment, houses, food, and other life needs.

- *Emotional gifts:* Present in people who are compassionate and understanding toward others' feelings; also creative geniuses.

- *Mental gifts:* Relates to individuals with high intellect and smartness; also people great with structure and project or data management.

- *Relational gifts:* Depicts people who inherently understand and respond to others' needs for love and healing.

- *Communicative gifts:* Describes those who excel at teaching, conveying philosophies, music, or writing.

- *Visual gifts:* Portrayed in people skilled in aesthetics, strategy, or planning.

- *Spiritual gifts:* Relates to those who comprehend and care about another's spiritual nature, purpose, or light.

STEP THREE: **Further Relate.** You can now ask to receive additional spiritual insights; if you can, converse with the subject until the conversation is complete.

STEP FOUR: **Close.** When you're finished, ask for healing streams to provide blessings, and continue with your day.

• EXERCISE 18 •

Lighting Up the Dark

What should you do if you sense that a dark being is interfering with the person or natural being you're empathizing with? Following are steps to take.

STEP ONE: **Conduct Spirit-to-Spirit.** If you suspect interference, immediately seek the Spirit. The Spirit will protect you and any and all subjects with healing streams.

STEP TWO: **Ask the Question.** Request that the Spirit show you if the subject of empathy is being interfered with. Affirmative responses might appear in the following ways:

- a feeling of heaviness or intense heat or cold

- a vision of the interference

- a message from the Spirit indicating that interference is present

- a spiritual awareness of the dark nature of being

As well, you might come up with a blank screen, which could indicate there isn't any interference. If this is the case, healing streams, especially white ones, can clear the process and return you to everyday engagements. Otherwise, continue.

STEP THREE: **Ask for Containment.** Request that the Spirit surround the negative being with healing streams so it can't further pollute you or the subject. If the Spirit chooses to completely remove the being at this point, it will. You'll sense a subsequent empty space, which the Spirit will fill with healing streams. Then ask the Spirit what else you need to know or do, and then close. If the encased dark being still remains, move to step four.

STEP FOUR: **Request Information.** What does the Spirit need you to know about this being? The Spirit will provide insights, sensations, messages, or visions to inform you about the type of being, indicate its reasons for intruding, show who it's directing its interference at, and relay what must be cleared. If appropriate, discuss matters with the subject of the interference.

STEP FIVE: **Release.** Ask the Spirit to remove the dark being from the subject or the situation and use healing streams to care for all concerned. Healing streams will repair any energetic holes and wounds. You can always ask for more white coloration to wash and caulk significant injury sites.

STEP SIX: **Close with Gratitude.** Thank the Spirit, and know that healing streams will remain connected to all concerned.

Spiritual Tips
Staying Light on Your Feet

There are several methods for keeping yourself open to spiritual insights. Some of these are age-old and have been used in spiritual forums across time. Others are more modern. Consider the following:

Fast

If medically approved, fasting can clear your mind and connect your spirit with your body. If you choose to fast or abstain from food for a day or a few hours, concentrate on matters of the heart and spirit while refraining from food.

Eat Chocolate

Small amounts of organic dark chocolate or raw cocoa are very grounding and activate psychic visions.

Pray

Prayer involves sending a communication to the Spirit. Create a need or question and compose a short prayer, relaying it to the Spirit with healing streams. You can then meditate for a response.

Meditate

To meditate is to be in a receptive state for a response to a prayer or an insight from the Spirit. Meditation doesn't need to require vast amounts of time. Instead, take a few minutes and perform Spirit-to-Spirit. Concentrate on the Spirit while gently breathing, and ask the Spirit to grant you a psychic image, verbal message, or awareness. You can also request that the Spirit provide you a sign, omen, dream, or other communiqué over the next few days. As well, you can journal and see what is revelatory through that.

It's now time to put all four forms of empathy together and apply them toward two major purposes: healing and manifesting.

Chapter Seven

EMPATHY FOR
HEALING AND MANIFESTING

ere you'll acquire several exercises that will mix all four types of spiritual empathy so you can perform both healing and manifesting. Although each of the four previous chapters included ways to connect with natural beings or the otherworldly, the main focus of this chapter will be human-to-human contact. I will, however, provide tips for assisting nonhuman communication.

In a nutshell, healing involves releasing energies that are inhibiting physical, psychological, or spiritual well-being. Manifesting promotes the achievement of needs and desires. Each of the four major exercises in this chapter will address one or the other goal. Specifically, the exercises will assist you with bonding with a subject, assessing and clearing another's issues from their past, addressing the subject's current life and needs, and helping the subject with future goals. Get ready to make an enduring difference in another's life.

• EXERCISE 19 •
Establishing a Bond

When we're empathically relating to another person, especially if we're providing healing or manifesting assistance, it's helpful to establish the strongest possible bond. Achieving this goal is best achieved by meeting the following criteria:

- figuring out what style or styles of empathy are relaying data
- deciding which style of communication will make the most sense to the subject
- using the language that mirrors the empathic style being employed
- pinpointing the time frame that the empathic data is indicating

Why are these factors so important? Imagine that you experience a strong physical reaction when a friend talks about a recent date. You feel punched in the gut. Since the indicators are physical, you assume that you're receiving a physically empathic message. You then conduct another sweep through your system and a deep sadness arises. The emotionally empathic senses were always there; you merely missed them the first time.

Which style will you mirror to the friend? It's vital to thoughtfully figure out not only how we're getting a message, but how we'll convey our impressions to a subject. After all, we want them to comprehend our feedback.

There isn't necessarily a correlation between the empathic style you're using and the language that will make sense to the subject. We all have different communication styles. Some of us identify with data better if it's presented in physically based terms; others resonate with emotional ideas. Yet others relate to spiritual concepts. And some individuals best comprehend visual or verbal communiqués.

The easiest way to assess the subject's style to ask questions, which you learned to do in exercise 14, "Creating the Curious Questioner." Although the exercise was devoted to mental empathy, the process of asking questions is useful during any empathic interrelating.

To explain, I'll return to the fist-in-the-stomach example.

In order to pinpoint the relevance of the empathic sensations, you can start a Q&A aloud with the subject, perhaps raising a question like this: "Is there a reason that my stomach is in pain right now, or am I picking up on something inside of you?" You could also ask, "I'm feeling sad when you talk about this. Are you sad about anything?"

These sorts of exchanges will help you hone in on the meaning of what you're receiving and check out your subject's relating style. If the subject lights up and relates to your physically based language, go there. If they stir at an emotional relating, use emotional terms. (See tip 19, "What to Say," for additional ideas.)

As for time frame, that gut punch could be describing a physical blow your friend received during the date, which occurred in the past. It might indicate her current emotional reaction to the man. It could also reference an event that could occur in the future. Maybe this man could actually hit your friend or emotionally wound her.

You can see why it's important to figure out these types of issues. Toward that end, I'll walk you through several steps as if conducting an assessment in real time with a person who is present. The tips that follow will help you apply these steps in various ways.

STEP ONE: **Become Aware.** As soon as you sense you're picking up an empathic message, breathe deeply and acknowledge the communication. Concentrate on the source of the data.

STEP TWO: **Perform Spirit-to-Spirit.** Affirm your own spirit, the subject's spirit, all beneficial spirits, and the Spirit. Turn the process over to the Spirit.

STEP THREE: **Assess the Communication.** Typify the empathic messages you are receiving.

- *Physical empathy:* These communiqués are body-based and feel pleasant or unpleasant.

- *Emotional empathy:* Emotional input stirs feelings such as anger, fear, sadness, disgust, or joy.

- *Mental empathy:* Mental messages are experienced as inexplicable knowledge about the subject's thoughts or perceptions.

- *Spiritual empathy:* When spiritually insightful, you'll be aware of what the Spirit knows about a person or what the Spirit wants them to attend to. You will be conscious of a spiritual need, sensitivity, gift, or spiritual nature. You might also attune to influences from a dark or light being.

While empathy provides the just-listed types of awareness, you might also access information that is psychically verbal or visual. Simply take these additional insights into account.

STEP FOUR: **Reassess the Communication.** Review the empathic message already received and label its style. Then check to see if there is data available through a different empathic style. Simply page through each one—physical, emotional, mental, and spiritual—to uncover additional information.

STEP FIVE: **Check Out Assumptions.** When ready, relay your impressions to the subject. Start by employing the language related to the style, using active verbs. I've provided ways to construct style-related promptings below:

- *Physical empathy:* Try filling in the beginning phrases, such as:

  When I attune to you, I...sense, smell, or physically feel or notice a pain, sensation, pleasantry, ache, etc.

  What I sense makes me want to...run, hit, move, touch, stop, start, etc.

- *Feeling empathy:* Select verbs that suit the beginning phrases:

  In relating to you, I feel...angry, sad, scared, disgusted, happy, etc.

  What I feel makes me want to...cry, scream, laugh, shout, become quiet, create, etc.

- *Mental empathy:* Add to the phrase provided.

  When connecting to you, I perceive a...
      thought, judgment, attitude, bias, perception, idea, motivation, desire, etc.

- *Spiritual empathy:* Select follow-on verbs like the following:

  *In relation to you, I'm aware of a...*higher knowing, wisdom, consciousness, etc.

  I sense a being present that makes me feel... scared, hopeful, insightful, heavy, etc.

As a note, good verbs for visual responses include these words: *see*, *picture*, *envision*, and *perceive*. Verbs related to verbal styles include terms like these: *hear*, *get*, *get wind of*, and *listen to*.

If the subject responds to the language style, continue to use it. If not, simply switch language styles until you strike a chord.

STEP SIX: **Arrive at a Deeper Interpretation.** You're now interrelating with the subject. Continue to bounce ideas back and forth, letting them add their explanations to your insights. You can use questions like those found in exercise 14, "Creating the Curious Questioner." Following are a few examples:

- What does my perception mean to you?
- How do you relate to what I'm saying?
- What is your take on what I'm sensing?
- Is there something you are comfortable sharing with me?
- Do you want me to keep relaying what I'm picking up?
- Is there more to the story you want to share?

STEP SEVEN: **Highlight the Time Frame.** Empathy is unbounded by time. As you're conversing with the subject, question the subject to pinpoint a time frame. You can also ask the Spirit for intuitive answers. Leading questions include the following:

- Does this data relate to the past? If so, how long ago? What events are important to remember?

- Is this information about the present? Does it describe a current situation or an awareness in this moment?

- Is this empathic insight future-oriented? Might it involve something that could possibly or probably occur? Should this event happen or is it supposed to be averted? What is to be done with this data?

STEP EIGHT: **Summarize.** Restate your conclusions aloud and ask the subject aloud, as well as the Spirit through your internal intuitive faculties, if there needs to be any follow-up activity by you or them.

STEP NINE: **Close.** Silently thank the Spirit for assisting you with this process. Aloud, thank the subject for honoring you with their honesty.

∞

What to Say

It can be helpful to have a few phrases ready to best enable bonding when empathizing. I'll jumpstart you with several ideas:

- I get you.
- Let me see if I understand.
- I'd love to better understand where you're coming from.
- I'm feeling a bit disconnected; what can I do?
- I'm sensing that something is going on with you; can you help me figure it out?
- Would you like my assistance with your concern?
- Is there something you are struggling with?
- I'm picking up a need; do you want us to explore it?

Make sure to come up with a few of your own too!

TIP 20

༄

Empathizing with a Natural Being Using All Four Gifts

What if you're receiving a message from a natural being? Employ all your empathic gifts, starting with spiritual empathy. Conduct Spirit-to-Spirit and ask that the Spirit bring you a spiritual guide to translate messages between you and the natural being. As a mediator, the being will assure you both understand your communiqués. Then see if there are also physical, emotional, or mental insights to be had. As always, request healing streams to establish solid empathic boundaries.

• EXERCISE 20 •
Clearing a Subject's Past Issues

How can you best support a subject with releasing or
healing an issue from their past after you've picked up on
a problem empathically? This exercise will assist.

The core of these steps involves using healing streams
to deliver transformational energies. The actual transport
of these energies, which are customized for the subject, is
managed by the Spirit, attending beings of light, or a subject's spirit. The streams will keep you separated from the
process. This means you won't absorb another's off energies, get overinvolved in the undertaking, or be tempted
to manipulate in order to make everything "all better."

STEP ONE: **Participate in the Empathizing Process—with Permission.** Once you've picked up
on another's empathic message, conduct Spirit-to-
Spirit. Employ exercise 19, "Establishing a Bond."
If you get the intuitive sense that something from
the past is bothering the subject, obtain verbal
permission from the subject to explore the topic.

There are times you can't request authoriza-
tion, such as if the subject is sick, in a coma, very
young or old, or unable to respond. You can then

request a go-ahead from their spirit or the Spirit. You'll sense, see, hear, or feel an acknowledgement. If you don't get approval, it's important to request healing streams and then release your involvement. Otherwise, you can continue.

STEP TWO: **Assess for History.** Ask the Spirit if there is a historical reason why the subject is requiring your empathic assistance. You might receive a physical, emotional, mental, or spiritual response. You might also get an image or a psychically verbal insight. If you don't get a message, ask for healing streams and release yourself from the process; otherwise, keep going.

STEP THREE: **Further Analyze the Issue.** It's time to probe for the causal issue. Ask internally to be intuitively shown the core issue, and pay attention to the ensuring flow of data, only interrupting to ask questions inside of your head. If the subject is present, run your ideas by them. Aloud, bat thoughts back and forth until you both seem clear about the issue and its effects.

STEP FOUR: **Ask for Healing Streams.** Once the assessment is complete, request that the Spirit send healing streams directly to the subject, not only in the present time, but also to their past self. The streams will keep the subject filled with power, grace, and healing and will remain in place as long as needed.

STEP FIVE: **Conclude.** If you're interrelating in real time, complete any conversation with the subject; otherwise, do so in your mind. Then ask the Spirit to employ healing streams to renew the empathic boundaries of all concerned. Thank the Spirit and return to your everyday functions when ready.

❧

Healing a Part of Yourself
Using All Four Gifts

If you sense that a part of you from the past requires assistance, use exercise 20, "Clearing a Subject's Past Issues," as a framework. Simply consider this part of yourself as the subject. Interrelate with this self as if it's a separate person. This is easiest to do if you imagine that self as separate from you and dwelling within the time period involved in the causal issue. You can also use pencil and paper and write to the historical part of yourself, communicating as if through instant messaging. This past self will be reintegrated in step four.

Transforming a Current Problem

When empathizing with another person, it's sometimes not enough to merely relate. We can also direct energy for transformation. The following steps are multilayered and will help you compose healing streams in four different ways: physically, emotionally, mentally, and spiritually. Using all four styles ensures that the healing streams will meet every healing need. After learning this technique, you can situationally mix and match healing streams. For instance, if someone is experiencing a physical problem, you can ask if you can touch them while focusing on healing streams. You could even make them something to eat or walk with them while directing healing streams.

Now get ready to create a healing.

STEP ONE: **Recognize a Need.** How can you tell if a subject has a healing need? First, see if the subject is sending out a call for help. You'll sense it as a bodily, emotional, mental, or spiritual awareness. You might also hear a verbal message or see a psychic image. Of course, the subject might verbally tell you!

STEP TWO: **Perform Spirit-to-Spirit/Get Permission.** Acknowledge your own spirit, the subject's spirit, the assisting spirits, and the Spirit. Ask the Spirit if you should participate in a healing for the subject. Proceed if you get a go-ahead, which might be felt as a strong yes in your body, an affirmative awareness, a positive emotion, or maybe even a psychic image depicting the words "go ahead." If you don't receive an affirmative, ask for healing streams to separate you and the subject, and continue with your previous interactions. Otherwise, move to the next step.

STEP THREE: **Request Assistance.** Request that the Spirit merge four different types of healing energies, which are described next, into a single stream of light.

- *Physical energies:* From the natural world, the Spirit gathers all the elements required to stimulate the physical alterations needed by the subject. You might sense, smell, or relate more to a specific element rather than another. Let the Spirit compose the correct concoction of the following elements from those described next.

Fire: Provides purification and the ignition of passion

Water: Soothes emotions and restores flow

Air: Grants ideas and needed information

Wood: Offers renewal and restores optimism

Metal: Bestows protection and deflects negativity

Earth: Affords fortification and rebuilding

Stone: Holds and shares history and strength

Ether: Carries spiritual principles and wisdom

Star: Blends fire and ether, creating impassioned philosophies

Sound: Delivers vibrations of power

Light: Shares vibrations of love

- *Emotional energies:* The Spirit or spiritual guides will select healing energies as represented by the following colors:

  Brown: Rootedness

  Red: Vitality

  Orange: Creativity

  Yellow: Power

  Blue: Communications

  Indigo: Spiritual knowledge

  Violet: Visions

  White: Purity

  Black: Ancient power

  Gold: Instant change

  Pink: Lovingkindness

- *Mental energies:* The highest of mental energetics are delivered as virtues, spiritual qualities that update our thinking and perceptions. With Spirit, choose from the following examples:

  Healing

  Goodness

Clarity

Hope

Honesty

Truth

Gratitude

Compassion

Courage

Prudence

Justice

- *Spiritual energies:* If deemed needed by the Spirit, various beings of the light might respond to the need, sprinkling their own magic dust. Following is a short list of these beings and what they can accomplish.

  Archangels: Deliver messages from the Spirit

  Seraphim: Restore holiness

  Cherubim: Guard and protect

  Principalities: Provide advice about leadership

  Virtues/Strongholds: Enable miracles

> **Dominions:** Carry the highest decrees from the heavens
>
> **Powers:** Transmute evil
>
> **Shining Ones:** Bring heaven to earth
>
> **Fairies:** Alter the natural world

STEP FOUR: **Send the Healing.** Request that the Spirit blend all four gathered energies into a star of light and deliver the result to the subject. Healing streams will transport this energetic antidote and remain attached and operable until the work is complete.

STEP FIVE: **Add a Final Blessing.** Request that the Spirit provide a final blessing to the subject and also renew your energy. Return to your world when ready.

• EXERCISE 22 •

Helping Someone Manifest a Desire

Sometimes an empathic connection stirs you to support another's desire. You might tune into their wish through a dream or during or after a conversation. I'll walk you through a start-to-finish process of manifesting.

STEP ONE: **Become Aware of a Desire.** If someone is openly discussing a wish or a dream, move to step two. What if you're picking up on on their wish empathically (or intuitively)? In this case, it's helpful to know the indicators. Following are a few clues:

Physical empathy: You'll feel the other's desire within your body. For instance, you might suddenly be gripped with the sensation that you are holding a skateboard, diamond ring, someone's hand, or a contract for a new job.

Emotional empathy: Emotionally empathic signs can include sensing the subject's sadness about what's missing, joy at the thought of a wish coming true, anger that a desire hasn't been fulfilled or supported, fear about not realizing a dream, or disgust about the beings, issues, or people preventing a desire's realization. You might also receive a psychically visual or verbal clue along with the empathic awareness. For instance, an image of a subject's aspiration might pop into your mind, perhaps with an accompanying emotion. You might hear words inside your mind, such as "he wants a kitten," along with the feeling of a cat being stroked.

Mental empathy: Mental empaths will perceive the subject's aspiration. Usually, you'll just sense what another desires in your gut. You might even believe that you're reading a subject's thoughts or sensing their hidden motivations. For instance, you might be speaking with a friend about cooking and realize that they want to own their own restaurant.

Spiritual empathy: Prophets attune to the other's spirit, or the greater Spirit, to know what the subject needs—or *should* need. You'll resonate with the desires of another's heart or the inclinations that could move them along their path of purpose. For instance, imagine that a friend is saying she wants to start a family. A niggling sensation might suggest she actually wants to travel first.

STEP TWO: **Carry out Spirit-to-Spirit.** Once you're knowingly tuning into a subject's desire, conduct

Spirit-to-Spirit. Affirm your own spirit, as well as the subject's spirit. Acknowledge the presence of any beings of light and request that the Spirit assist with the manifesting.

STEP THREE: **Become Clearer.** It's time to become clearer about the subject's desire. If the subject is at hand, ask permission aloud. If they aren't, ask the Spirit to authorize this exploration. If you get a no from either party, ask for healing streams and separate from the process. If it's deemed okay to move ahead, ask the Spirit to provide insights. Open to images, insights, impressions, and knowledge. Share your knowledge with the subject, if applicable, and ask for feedback.

STEP FOUR: **Infuse with Healing Streams.** When you feel like you've acquired at least bare-bones information, ask the Spirit to support the subject's dream with healing streams. The streams of light will be delivered directly to the subject, whose desire will be fortified and assisted. The streams will remain attached and beneficial for as long as needed.

STEP FIVE: **Close.** When finished, ask the Spirit to continue blessing the subject and return to your life.

TIP 22

Programming a Stone for Manifesting

Manifesting energies supportive of a subject's dream can be programmed into a stone, which a subject can then carry, wear, or gaze at to better achieve their desire. Select a stone that best suits the other's wish.

To program a stone, perform Spirit-to-Spirit and request that the Spirit infuse it with the healing streams needed to boost the desire. Let the streams then seal the stone. Give the stone to the subject. The healing streams will continually cleanse and renew the stone.

Following is a list you can use to select a stone. How do you use this list? If the subject wants to lose weight, you might select an agate, which relates to nourishment. If they need money, you might choose an emerald, which resonates with abundance.

Now let's examine a few stones:

AGATE	NOURISHMENT
AMBER	WELL-BEING
AMETHYST	SPIRITUAL PROTECTION
CARNELIAN	SENSUALITY
DIAMOND	HIGHEST AND MOST DIFFICULT OF DESIRES TO ACHIEVE
EMERALD	ABUNDANCE
FLUORITE	FOCUS
GARNET	SELF-HEALING
HEMATITE	GROUNDING
LAPIS LAZULI	TRUTH
OBSIDIAN	PURIFICATION
OPAL	EMOTIONAL AMPLIFICATION
PEARL	LOVE AND FRIENDSHIP
QUARTZ	SPIRITUAL DESIRES
ROSE QUARTZ	LOVE
RUBY	PASSION
SAPPHIRE	COMMUNICATION SKILLS
TURQUOISE	RELATING TO HIGHER SPIRITS

TIP 23

❧

Asking a Guide to Help with Manifesting

When we're led by a subject or the Spirit, we can request that the Spirit assign the subject a special guide to help them manifest a specific desire. Perform Spirit-to-Spirit and ask the Spirit to surround the subject with healing streams and to then provide them with a spiritual consultant or guide. Either you, the subject (if present), or both might sense the presence of this being. If so, share with each other.

One of my favorite activities is to request a fairy godmother or a fairy godfather. The last time I did this, a woman who hadn't dated for ten years was asked out by a man at work. After a year, they were married. They were perfect for each other.

CONCLUSION

Y ou are empathic! In fact, science is proving that we are all hard-wired for empathy, the ability to connect with others. But that's only the beginning of the story.

As you learned in this book, empathy is—and is more than—a neurological process. It actually involves an energetic exchange through which two types of energy, which is vibrating information, transfer between two or more people or beings. Physical energy, one of the types, is measurable. Concretely, empathic messages are produced by the mirror neurons and electromagnetic fields of the person or being desiring empathic attention. This information is then registered within the body of the empathic recipient and invites a response.

Subtle energy, the other form of energy, is more slippery. Also called psychic, spiritual, intuitive, or mystical energy, it is transmitted from one being to another so fast that the conveyance is nearly instant. And although subtle energy is registered in the physical body, it is mainly authorized by the subtle body, which is composed of a variety of subtle organs, channels, and fields.

All empathic messages can be divided into four main types: physical, emotional, mental, and spiritual. Though the body is always involved in receiving, interpreting, and responding to empathic information, most of the messages are subtle. This is why we can easily become overwhelmed with a subject's empathic communication. But we can also fall prey to two other negative empathic tendencies. We can become underempathic, which involves closing off to one or more styles of empathic information. Or we can employ our empathy to manipulate others or be vulnerable to being deceived by the manipulated. Because of these empathic challenges, it's important to have healthy empathic boundaries, which are programmed by our internal beliefs.

Most of this book was devoted to exploring ways to safely develop and apply the four empathic abilities, using concepts and techniques that afford the evaluating and establishment of empathic boundaries. You also learned how to blend the four styles for healing and manifesting. Look at how empowered you've become as an empath!

You can sense another's physical sensations in your own body but also ease their pain. You can feel their feelings as well as provide ease. You can acknowledge their perceptions and spiritual gifts while enhancing both. And you can do this and more for another person and also for a part of yourself, a pet, and even a plant.

I've only one more suggestion. Go beyond the last page of this book. Next time you pick a flower, infuse your entire body with its aroma. In fact, let in the flower's color, purpose, and ideas. As Shakespeare would advise, "be" the flower. When petting your dog, surrender into the love being sent to you. And when someone you're empathizing with has a need, give. Give love. For it is love that motivates empathy and empathy that creates more love.

BIBLIOGRAPHY

Anderson, Cameron, and Dacher Keltner. 2002. "The Role of Empathy in the Formation and Maintenance of Social Bonds." *Behavioral and Brain Sciences* 5, no. 1 (February). https://philpapers.org/rec/ANDTRO-5.

Bergland, Christopher. 2013. "The Neuroscience of Empathy." *Psychology Today*, October 10, 2013. www.psychologytoday.com/us/blog/the-athletes-way/201310/the-neuroscience-empathy.

Blake, William. "The Tyger." Poetry Foundation.
    https://www.poetryfoundation.org
        /poems/43687/the-tyger.

Bonn, Scott. 2014. "How to Tell a Sociopath from a
    Psychopath." *Psychology Today*, January 22, 2014.
    www.psychologytoday.com/us/blog/wicked
        -deeds/201401/how-tell-sociopath-psychopath.

Center for Building a Culture of Empathy. n.d. "Benefits of
    Empathy."
    http://cultureofempathy.com/References/Benefits/.

Exploring Your Mind. 2018. "Theory of Mind: The Root of
    Empathy." February 26, 2018.
    https://exploringyourmind.com
        /theory-mind-root-empathy/.

Georgiou, Aristosos. 2018. "Honeybees Understand the
    Complex Mathematical Concept of Zero." *Newsweek*,
    June 7, 2018.
    http://www.newsweek.com/honeybees-understand
        -complex-mathematical-concept-zero-964632.

Gregoire, Carolyn. 2017. "People with This Condition
    Literally Feel What Others Are Feeling." *Huffpost*,
    February 8, 2017.
    www.huffingtonpost.com/entry/mirror-touch
        -synesthesia _us_589a2207e4b040613139cb3a.

HeartMath Institute. 2018. "Study Shows Geomagnetic Fields and Solar Activity Affect Human Autonomic Nervous System Function." April 11, 2018. https://www.heartmath.org/articles-of-the -heart/study-shows-geomagnetic-fields -solar-activity-affect-human-autonomic -nervous-system-functions/.

———. 2019. "Science of the Heart." https://www.heartmath.org/research/science-of-the -heart/energetic-communication/.

———. 2016. "Interconnectivity Research Project." June 29, 2016. https://www.heartmath.org/calendar-of-events /interconnectivity-tree-research-project/.

Killam, Kasley. 2014. "Building Empathy in Healthcare." *Mind & Body*, October 27, 2014. https://greatergood.berkeley.edu/article/item /building_empathy_in_healthcare.

Lehrer, Jonah, ed. 2008. "The Mirror Neuron Revolution." *Scientific American*, July 1, 2008. https://www.scientificamerican.com/article/the -mirror-neuron-revolut/.

Light, Sharee, and James Coan. 2009. "Empathy Is Associated with Dynamic Change in Preffront Brain Electrical Activity During Positive Emotion in Children." *Child Development*, July/August 2009. https://centerhealthyminds.org/assets/files -publications/LightEmpathyChildDevelopment.pdf.

McDonald, Hal. 2016. "I Feel Your Pain (Literally)."
　　Psychology Today, October 2016.
　　　https://www.psychologytoday.com/us/blog/time
　　　　-travelling-apollo/201610/i-feel-your-pain-literally.

McTaggart, Lynne. 2008. *The Field*. New York: Harper
　　Perennial.

Panayotova, Liya. 2017. "5 Suprising Ways Empathy Can
　　Change Your Life." *Paste*, February 9, 2017.
　　　www.pastemagazine.com/articles/2017/01/5
　　　　-surprising-ways-empathy-will-change
　　　　-your-life.html.

Phys.Org. 2011. "Research Raises New Questions about
　　Animal Empathy." *Washington State University*,
　　December 8, 2011.
　　　https://phys.org/news/2011-12-animal
　　　　-empathy.html.

Quora. n.d. "What Percentage of the Light Spectrum Are
　　Humans Able to See with Their Eyes?"
　　　https://www.quora.com/What-percentage-of-the
　　　　-light-spectrum-are-humans-able-to-see-with
　　　　-their-eyes.

Ratner, Paul. 2017. "Empathy Can Be Hazardous to Your
　　Health, Finds Study." *Bigthink*, October 2, 2017.
　　　http://bigthink.com/paul-ratner/empathy-can-be
　　　　-hazardous-to-your-health.

Ripper, Sarah. 2017. "Plant Neurobiology Shows How Trees Are Just Like Humans." *Uplift*, February 27, 2017.
https://upliftconnect.com/plant-neurobiology-trees-humans/.

Safina, Carl. 2016. *Beyond Words*. New York: Picador.

Sandoiu, Ana. 2018. "How Much of Our Empathy Is Down to Genes?" *MedicalNewsToday*, March 2018.
https://www.medicalnewstoday.com/articles/321173.php.

Schmitz, Terry. 2016. "Empathy—The Cornerstone of Emotional Intelligence." May 16, 2016.
https://www.conovercompany.com/empathy-the-cornerstone-of-emotional-intelligence/.

Science Friday. 2014. "New Research on Plant Intelligence May Forever Change How You Think About Plants." January 10, 2014.
https://www.pri.org/stories/2014-01-09/new-research-plant-intelligence-may-forever-change-how-you-think-about-plants.

Stone, Jerry. 2016. "The Importance of Empathy in Healthcare." *Medical GPS*, December 13, 2016.
http://blog.medicalgps.com/the-importance-of-empathy-in-healthcare.

Strain, George. 2017. "How Well Do Dogs and Other Animals Hear?" April 10, 2017.
http://www.lsu.edu/deafness/HearingRange.html.

Taylor, Ben. n.d. "Machiavellianism, Cognition, and Emotion." *PsychCentral.* https://psychcentral.com/lib/machiavellianism-cognition-and-emotion-understanding-how-the-machiavellian-thinks-feels-and-thrives/.

GET MORE AT LLEWELLYN.COM

Visit us online to browse hundreds of our books and decks, plus sign up to receive our e-newsletters and exclusive online offers.

- Free tarot readings • Spell-a-Day • Moon phases
- Recipes, spells, and tips • Blogs • Encyclopedia
- Author interviews, articles, and upcoming events

GET SOCIAL WITH LLEWELLYN

Find us on   @LlewellynBooks

www.Facebook.com/LlewellynBooks

GET BOOKS AT LLEWELLYN

LLEWELLYN ORDERING INFORMATION

Order online: Visit our website at www.llewellyn.com to select your books and place an order on our secure server.

Order by phone:
- Call toll free within the US at 1-877-NEW-WRLD (1-877-639-9753)
- We accept VISA, MasterCard, American Express, and Discover.

Order by mail:
Send the full price of your order (MN residents add 6.875% sales tax) in US funds plus postage and handling to: Llewellyn Worldwide, 2143 Wooddale Drive, Woodbury, MN 55125-2989

POSTAGE AND HANDLING

STANDARD (US): (Please allow 12 business days)
$30.00 and under, add $6.00.
$30.01 and over, FREE SHIPPING.

CANADA:
We cannot ship to Canada. Please shop your local bookstore or Amazon Canada.

INTERNATIONAL:
Customers pay the actual shipping cost to the final destination, which includes tracking information.

Visit us online for more shipping options.
Prices subject to change.

FREE CATALOG!

To order, call 1-877-NEW-WRLD ext. 8236 or visit our website